Writing Empirical Research Reports

A Basic Guide for Students of the Social and Behavioral Sciences

Seventh Edition

Fred Pyrczak

California State University, Los Angeles

Randall R. Bruce

Editorial Consultant

Pyrczak Publishing

P.O. Box 250430 ❖ Glendale, CA 91225

"Pyrczak Publishing" is an imprint of Fred Pyrczak, Publisher, A California Corporation.

Although the author and publisher have made every effort to ensure the accuracy and completeness of information contained in this book, we assume no responsibility for errors, inaccuracies, omissions, or any inconsistency herein. Any slights of people, places, or organizations are unintentional.

Project Director: Monica Lopez.

Editorial assistance provided by Cheryl Alcorn, Jerry Buchanan, Jenifer Dill, Karen Disner, Brenda Koplin, Jack Petit, Erica Simmons, and Sharon Young.

Cover design by Robert Kibler and Larry Nichols.

Printed in the United States of America by Malloy, Inc.

ISBN 1-884585-97-3

Contents

Notes

Introduction to the Seventh Edition

This text presents guidelines frequently followed by writers of empirical research reports. The guidelines describe the types of information that should be included, how this information should be expressed, and where various types of information should be placed within a research report.

Students whose professors require them to write research-based term papers that resemble journal articles will find this text useful. The exercises at the end of each chapter are designed for their use. Graduate students who are writing theses and dissertations will find that the guidelines also apply to their writing. Interspersed throughout the text are pointers for such students.

Assumptions Underlying This Text

It is assumed that students have a traditional style manual such as the *Publication Manual of the American Psychological Association* (APA), which prescribes mechanical details for research writing. It is also assumed that students have already selected an important research topic, applied sound research methods, and analyzed the data. Thus, these topics are not covered.

Considerations in Using This Text

The guidelines presented in this text are based on generalizations that the authors reached while reading extensively in journals in the social and behavioral sciences. If you are a student using this text in a research class, your professor may ask you to modify some of the guidelines you will find here. This may occur for two reasons. First, as a learning experience, a professor may require students to do certain things that go beyond the preparation of a paper for possible publication. For instance, we suggest that the literature review for a journal article should usually be highly selective. However, a professor may require students to write extensive literature reviews to show that they can conduct a comprehensive search of the literature on a topic. Second, as in all types of writing, there is a certain amount of subjectivity concerning what constitutes effective writing; even experts differ. Fortunately, these differences are less pronounced in scientific writing than in many other types of writing.

Experienced writers may violate many of the guidelines presented in this text and still write effective research reports that are publishable. Beginners are encouraged to follow the guidelines rather closely until they have mastered the art of scientific writing.

continued

Where to Begin in This Text

For a quick overview of five fundamental principles for effective research writing, begin with Appendix B, *Thinking Straight and Writing That Way*. Then read Chapter 1, which will provide an overview of the structure of typical research reports.

About the Examples in This Text

Most of the guidelines are illustrated with examples from research reports published in journals. References for these examples are indicated with footnotes. Complete bibliographic references can be found in the References section near the end of this book. Examples without footnotes were written by these authors to illustrate selected guidelines.

About the Seventh Edition

The most important change from the Sixth to the Seventh Edition is the modification of material throughout the book to increase consistency with the 2010 edition of the *Publication Manual of the American Psychological Association*. In addition, more than 30 new examples from published research reports have been added.

Acknowledgments

The authors are grateful to Dr. Dean Purcell of Oakland University; Dr. Robert Morman of California State University, Los Angeles; and Dr. Richard Rasor of American River College—all of whom provided many helpful comments on the various editions of this book.

Chapter 1
Structuring a Research Report

This chapter provides an overview of the elements typically included in research reports. Each of these is discussed in greater detail in later chapters.

➢ Guideline 1.1 A research report typically has a brief title.

Titles of published research reports are typically brief. They usually refer to the population of interest and to the variables studied. Example 1.1.1 shows a title of about average length for a research report published in an academic journal. In it, the variables are self-concept and employment status. The population consists of individuals with epilepsy.

Example 1.1.1
The Relationship Between Self-Concept and Employment Status Among Individuals With Epilepsy

Writing titles is discussed in more detail in Chapter 5.

➢ Guideline 1.2 An abstract usually follows the title.

An *abstract* is a brief summary of the research. It is often stated in 150 to 250 words. A typical abstract summarizes the purpose of the study, the methods used to conduct the research, and the results.

An abstract should normally be written after the body of the report has been completed. Hence, guidelines for writing abstracts are presented near the end of this book in Chapter 13.

➢ Guideline 1.3 The body of a typical research report begins with a literature review, which serves as the introduction to the research project.

In research reports published in academic journals, the literature review is presented just below the abstract. Literature is cited in order to (1) establish the importance of the research problem, (2) inform the readers about what is known and what is not known about the problem, and (3) establish the need for the research described in the rest of the research report. The literature review concludes with a statement of the specific research hypotheses or purposes.

In theses and dissertations, the literature review serves the same purposes as the literature review in reports of research in journals. However, it is traditional to begin a thesis or dissertation with an introduction in the first chapter, which presents the researcher's rationale for conducting the study and has relatively few citations to literature. This is followed by a second chapter that presents the literature review.

Writing introductions and literature reviews is covered in Chapter 6. Writing research hypotheses and objectives is covered in Chapters 2–4.

➢ Guideline 1.4 The Method section describes the participants, the measures, and other details on how the research was conducted.

The Method section immediately follows the literature review. At a minimum, it has two subheadings: "Participants" (sometimes called "Sample") and "Measures" (sometimes called "Instrumentation").

The subsection on the participants describes how they were identified and selected. The subsection on measures describes the instruments (e.g., tests, attitude scales, interview schedules) that were used to collect the data.

A third (optional) subheading, "Procedure," is sometimes included. This is the appropriate place to describe the treatments given in an experiment or any other steps taken to execute the research that were not already described under "Participants" or "Measures."

A fourth (optional) subheading, "Analysis," is sometimes included. This is used to discuss the selection of methods of analysis.[1]

Guidelines for writing Method sections are described in Chapters 9 and 10 and the first part of Chapter 11.

Example 1.4.1 shows the structure of a basic research report with the elements discussed up to this point in this chapter.

Example 1.4.1

Title in Upper- and Lowercase Letters
Abstract (a main heading; centered in bold)[2]
A literature review that introduces the research problem (with no heading)
Method (a main heading; centered in bold)
Participants (a subheading; flush left in bold)
Measures (a subheading; flush left in bold)
Procedure (optional; a subheading; flush left in bold)
Analysis (optional; a subheading; flush left in bold)

---

[1] This subheading is most common in reports on qualitative research (see Chapter 14) because methods for qualitative analysis are not standardized. In quantitative research reports, the selection of a standard method of statistical analysis usually does not need to be discussed.

[2] This heading should usually be used in unpublished papers. In research journals, it is often omitted, with the abstract being identified by its placement at the beginning and by being indented on the left and right.

➤ Guideline 1.5   The Results section presents the findings.

The Results section immediately follows the Method section. It has a major heading of "Results" and is centered. (See Example 1.7.1.)

In reports on quantitative research, the Results section is usually brief. Often, statistics are presented in tables (i.e., rows and columns of statistics) with a discussion of how they shed light on the research hypotheses or purposes.

In reports on qualitative research, the Results section can be lengthy. In this section, qualitative researchers describe the major themes revealed by the participants' responses. These are usually illustrated with direct quotations from the participants.

Chapter 11 describes how to write Results sections, and Chapter 14 examines writing results for qualitative research in more detail.

➤ Guideline 1.6   The Discussion section presents the researcher's interpretations.

The Discussion section immediately follows the Results section. It has a major heading of "Discussion" and is centered.[3] (See Example 1.7.1.) In long research reports, the discussion might begin with a brief summary of the methods and results of the research. In addition, researchers use this section to reflect on the results and their relationship to the research hypotheses and purposes. This section also often includes (1) a statement of the limitations of the research (i.e., weaknesses in the research methodology), (2) implications of the findings, and (3) suggested directions for future research.

Guidelines for writing the Discussion section are described in Chapter 12.

➤ Guideline 1.7   The reference list should contain references only to literature cited in the report.

The references are listed under the main heading "References" (centered in bold). The reference list should not be a suggested reading list. It should contain references only to literature cited in the research report. The preparation of a reference list is described in Chapter 15.

Example 1.7.1 shows the structure of a basic research report (without the optional subheadings discussed under Guideline 1.4).

---

[3] While this section can have various names, such as "Discussion and Conclusions," "Summary and Discussion," and "Discussion and Implications," the one-word heading "Discussion" is the most common.

Example 1.7.1

Title in Upper- and Lowercase Letters
Abstract (a main heading; centered in bold)
A literature review that introduces the research problem (with no heading)
Method (a main heading; centered in bold)
Participants (a subheading; flush left in bold)
Measures (a subheading; flush left in bold)
Results (a main heading; centered in bold)
Discussion (a main heading; centered in bold)
References (a main heading; centered in bold)

Note that the technical name for a main heading is *first-level heading*, while the technical name for a subheading under a main heading is *second-level heading*. Headings under a second-level heading are called *third-level headings*, which are discussed under the next guideline.

➤ **Guideline 1.8 In long reports, use additional second-level and third-level headings.**

In long research reports (or long sections within reports), consider using additional headings to guide readers. For instance, in a long Discussion section, these second-level headings might be used: "Summary," "Limitations," "Implications," and "Directions for Future Research."

Third-level headings might be used under second-level ones. For instance, under the second-level heading of "Measures," these third-level headings might be used: "Construction of the Measures," "Validity of the Measures," and "Administration of the Measures."

The three levels of headings for the Method section of a research report are illustrated in Example 1.8.1. Note that third-level headings end with a period.

Example 1.8.1

Method (a *first-level* heading; centered in bold)
Participants (a *second-level* heading; flush left in bold)
Measures (a *second-level* heading; flush left in bold)
Construction of the Measures. (a *third-level* heading; indented in bold)
Validity of the Measures. (a *third-level* heading; indented in bold)
Administration of the Measures. (a *third-level* heading; indented in bold)

As a general rule, longer sections of research reports should have more second- and third-level headings than shorter sections.

Concluding Comments

The essential elements in a research report are the title, abstract, introduction, literature review, a description of research methods, a section that presents results, and a discussion. Additional headings and subheadings may be used as needed for clarity.

Note that researchers also present definitions as well as descriptions of their assumptions in their research reports. These may be integrated within various sections of a report. Guidelines for writing these elements are presented in Chapters 7–8.

Exercise for Chapter 1

PART A

1. Titles of research reports usually refer to what two elements?

2. What is an "abstract"?

3. "An abstract usually consists of 500 words or more." According to this chapter, is this statement true *or* false?

4. According to this chapter, literature is cited in order to establish the importance of the research problem and to inform the readers about what is known and what is not known about the problem. It is also cited in order to do what else?

5. At a minimum, the Method section has what two subheadings (second-level headings)?

6. The Measures subsection describes what?

7. The Results section immediately follows what other section?

8. Suggested directions for future research are presented in which section?

PART B: Examine two reports of research published in journals, and answer the following questions.

9. Were the titles and abstracts "brief" *or* "lengthy"? Explain.

10. Were the headings and subheadings consistent with what you expected based on your reading of this chapter? Explain.

PART C: If you will be writing a thesis or dissertation in the near future, examine one and answer the following questions.

11. Are the introduction and literature review presented in separate chapters?

12. List all the chapter titles. Do they correspond to the headings described in this chapter?

Chapter 2
Writing Simple Research Hypotheses

Often, the purpose of a research project is to test a research hypothesis (i.e., gather data that shed light on the validity of a hypothesis).

In a single sentence, a simple research hypothesis describes the results that a researcher expects to find. In effect, it is a prediction. The following are guidelines for writing this type of hypothesis.

> ➤ **Guideline 2.1 A simple research hypothesis should name two variables and indicate the type of relationship expected between them.**

In Example 2.1.1, the variables are "psychomotor coordination" and "self-esteem." The researcher expects to find higher self-esteem among individuals with better psychomotor coordination as well as lower self-esteem among those with less coordination.

Example 2.1.1

There is a direct relationship between level of psychomotor coordination and degree of self-esteem.

In Example 2.1.2, "length of light deprivation" is a stimulus or independent variable, which will be manipulated by the researcher. The hypothesis suggests that some rats will be deprived of light for longer than others. The second variable is "performance in a maze task," which is an outcome or dependent variable. The hypothesis indicates that the researcher expects to find longer periods of light deprivation associated with poorer maze performance.

Example 2.1.2

Among rats, length of light deprivation from birth is inversely associated with performance in a maze task.

Example 2.1.3 also contains an independent variable: the type of homework assignment (Internet versus traditional). The anticipated relationship of this variable to students' enthusiasm for doing homework is clear in the hypothesis. Note that the students' enthusiasm for doing homework is the dependent variable (i.e., outcome).

Example 2.1.3

Students who are administered self-correcting homework assignments via the Internet have more enthusiasm for doing homework than students who are given traditional homework assignments.

In Example 2.1.4, two variables are named, but the expected relationship between them is not stated. The improved version of Example 2.1.4 makes it clear that the researcher believes that those with more free-floating anxiety have less ability to form friendships.

Example 2.1.4

College students differ in their levels of free-floating anxiety, and they differ in their ability to form friendships.

Improved Version of Example 2.1.4

Among college students, there is an inverse relationship between level of free-floating anxiety and ability to form friendships.

➢ Guideline 2.2   When there is an independent variable, name a specific dependent variable.

As indicated in the previous guideline, some studies have independent variables, which are sets of treatments that are manipulated by researchers. The outcome that results from a set of treatments is known as the dependent variable. The purpose of such a study (known as an experiment) is to determine the effects of the independent variable on the dependent variable.

The hypothesis for an experiment should name a specific dependent variable. In Example 2.2.1, the independent variable is the use of guest speakers. Furthermore, the term *more effective* implies that there is a dependent variable, which is not specified. The improved version specifies that the dependent variable is the number of career choices the participants are willing to consider.

Example 2.2.1

Career counseling supplemented with guest speakers holding various occupations is more effective than career counseling without guest speakers.

Improved Version of Example 2.2.1

Participants receiving career counseling supplemented with guest speakers holding various occupations are willing to consider a larger number of career choices than participants who receive career counseling without guest speakers.

Because the purpose of all experiments is to determine the effects of the independent variable on a dependent variable, it is never sufficiently specific to state only that the dependent variable will have an *effect* or any variation on this term such as *more effective*. In other words, the specific behavior that will be used to judge effectiveness (e.g., number of career choices considered) should be explicitly mentioned.

Example 2.2.2 also fails to name a specific dependent variable (i.e., "better off" is not specific). The improved version specifies that "lower blood-pressure readings" is the dependent variable.

Example 2.2.2

Middle-aged males who regularly exercise vigorously are better off than those who do not exercise vigorously.

Improved Version of Example 2.2.2

Middle-aged males who regularly exercise vigorously have lower blood-pressure readings than those who do not exercise vigorously.

➢ Guideline 2.3 Consider naming population(s) in the hypothesis.

This guideline is especially applicable when (1) a relationship is expected only in a particular population, (2) the study deals with a population that previously has been unstudied, and (3) the focus of the study is on the comparison of two or more populations.

In Example 2.3.1, "young children" are identified as the researcher's population of interest.

Example 2.3.1

Among young children, there is a direct relationship between level of psychomotor coordination and degree of self-esteem.

In Example 2.3.2, "student nurses" are identified as the researcher's population of interest.

Example 2.3.2

Student nurses who receive computer-assisted training in calculating drug dosages make fewer calculation errors than student nurses who do not receive computer-assisted training.

In Example 2.3.3, two populations of high school students that will be compared (i.e., those with private transportation and those who use public transportation) are named in the hypothesis.

Example 2.3.3

High school students who have private transportation participate in more extracurricular activities than high school students who take public transportation.

➢ Guideline 2.4 A simple hypothesis should usually be expressed in a single sentence.

The hypothesis in Example 2.4.1 violates this guideline because it is stated in two sentences. This is corrected in the improved version.

Example 2.4.1

Social anxiety may impede the speech-giving performance of college students in speech communication classes. As a result, students with such anxiety will perform more poorly in such classes.

Improved Version of Example 2.4.1

Students with high levels of social anxiety exhibit poorer speech-giving performance than students with low levels of social anxiety.

➢ Guideline 2.5 Even a simple hypothesis should be as specific as possible within a single sentence.

The improved version of Example 2.5.1 is more specific than the original because the meaning of "computer use" (i.e., use of e-mail) and the meaning of "well-being" (i.e., reported levels of loneliness) are indicated in the improved version.

Example 2.5.1

There is an inverse relationship between computer use and well-being among the elderly.

Improved Version of Example 2.5.1

There is an inverse relationship between elderly individuals' use of e-mail and their reported levels of loneliness.

Likewise, the improved version of Example 2.5.2 is more specific than the original version because the improved version indicates that being "better administrators" will be measured in terms of employees' perceptions of leadership qualities. Also, the improved version is more specific because it indicates that two types of administrators will be compared.

Example 2.5.2

Administrators who provide wellness programs for their employees are perceived as better administrators.

Improved Version of Example 2.5.2

Administrators who provide wellness programs for their employees receive higher employee ratings on selected leadership qualities than administrators who do not provide wellness programs.

Deciding how specific to make a hypothesis is a subjective matter because it is usually not possible to provide full definitions of all terms in the single sentence that states a hypothesis. Instead, complete definitions should be provided elsewhere in a research report. Guidelines for writing definitions are presented in Chapter 7.

➤ Guideline 2.6 If a comparison is to be made, the elements to be compared should be stated.

Comparisons start with terms such as *more*, *less*, *higher*, and *lower*. Be sure to complete any comparisons that start with these terms. The comparison that is started in Example 2.6.1 is not complete, forcing the reader to make an assumption about the group(s) to which the low-achieving students will be compared. The improved versions are superior because they complete the comparison that starts with the word *more*. Note that the improved versions illustrate that the comparison can be completed in more than one way, clearly showing that the original version is vague.

Example 2.6.1

Low-achieving primary-grade students are more dependent on adults for psychological support.

Improved Versions of Example 2.6.1

Low-achieving primary-grade students are more dependent on adults for psychological support than are average achievers.

Low-achieving primary-grade students are more dependent on adults for psychological support than are low-achieving intermediate grade students.

➤ Guideline 2.7 Because most hypotheses deal with the behavior of groups, plural forms should usually be used.

In Example 2.7.1, singular terms are used to refer to the participants (i.e., "a husband" and "a wife"). Because the hypothesis will undoubtedly be tested using groups of husbands and wives, the improved version of the hypothesis below is preferable.

Example 2.7.1

Retirement satisfaction is greater when a husband or a wife has greater marital satisfaction than when he or she has less marital satisfaction.

Improved Version of Example 2.7.1

Individuals who have greater marital satisfaction have greater retirement satisfaction than those with less marital satisfaction.

➢ Guideline 2.8   Avoid sex-role stereotypes in the statement of a hypothesis.

In Example 2.8.1, use of the term "her level" reflects the sex-role stereotype that nursing is an occupation for women only. The problem has been corrected in the improved version by substituting the plural terms "nurses" and "their level." Of course, it is important to avoid sex-role stereotyping throughout research reports.

Example 2.8.1

There is a direct relationship between a nurse's participation in administrative decision-making and her level of job satisfaction.

Improved Version of Example 2.8.1

There is a direct relationship between nurses' participation in administrative decision-making and their level of job satisfaction.

➢ Guideline 2.9   A hypothesis should be free of terms and phrases that do not add to its meaning.

The improved version of Example 2.9.1 is much shorter than the original version, yet its meaning is clear.

Example 2.9.1

Among elementary school teachers, those who are teaching in year-round schools have higher morale than those who are teaching in elementary schools that follow a more traditional school-year schedule.

Improved Version of Example 2.9.1

Elementary school teachers who teach in year-round schools have higher morale than those who teach on a traditional schedule.

➢ Guideline 2.10   A hypothesis should indicate what will actually be studied—not the possible implications of a study or value judgments of the author.

In Example 2.10.1, the author is expressing a value judgment rather than the anticipated relationship between the variables to be studied. The improved version indicates how religion will be treated as a variable (i.e., attendance at religious services) and indicates the specific outcome (i.e., cheating behavior) that will be studied.

Example 2.10.1

Religion is good for society.

Improved Version of Example 2.10.1

Attendance at religious services is inversely associated with students' cheating behavior while taking classroom tests.

Note that if the hypothesis in the improved version of Example 2.10.1 is supported by the data generated to test the hypothesis, the researcher may want to assert that less cheating is "good for society" in his or her research report. Such an assertion is acceptable as long as the researcher makes it clear that the assertion is a value judgment and not a data-based conclusion.

➢ Guideline 2.11   A hypothesis usually should name variables in the order in which they occur or will be measured.

In Example 2.11.1, the natural order has been reversed because the deprivation will precede, and possibly produce, the anticipated anxiety. This problem has been corrected in the improved version.

Example 2.11.1

More free-floating anxiety is observed among adults who are subjected to longer periods of sensory deprivation.

Improved Version of Example 2.11.1

Adults who are subjected to extended periods of sensory deprivation experience more free-floating anxiety than those exposed to less deprivation.

In Example 2.11.2, the natural order has been reversed. Because political advertising precedes winning elections, advertisements should be mentioned before election to office. The problem has been corrected in the improved version.

Example 2.11.2

Politicians who win elective offices tend to focus their political advertisements on a limited number of issues, while those who lose elections tend to focus on a larger number of issues.

Improved Version of Example 2.11.2

Politicians who focus their political advertisements on a limited number of issues are more likely to win elective office than those whose advertisements cover a larger number of issues.

Of course, the researcher would be expected to define at some point in the research report what is meant by "limited number" and "larger number."

➢ Guideline 2.12 Avoid using the words *significant* or *significance* in a hypothesis.

The terms *significant* and *significance* usually refer to tests of statistical significance. Because most quantitative studies include these tests, reference to them in hypotheses is not necessary because knowledgeable readers can be assumed to know that the issue of statistical significance will be dealt with in the Results section of a quantitative research report.

Example 2.12.1 shows a hypothesis with the word *significantly* struck out because it is not necessary (nor is it standard) to include it.

Example 2.12.1

Adults who are subjected to extended periods of sensory deprivation experience ~~significantly~~ more free-floating anxiety than those exposed to less deprivation.

➢ Guideline 2.13 Avoid using the word *prove* in a hypothesis.

Empirical research does not prove its outcomes for three primary reasons. First, empirical research is usually based only on samples from populations, and it is safe to assume that no sample is perfectly representative of its population. Second, it is safe to assume that no test or other measurement procedure is perfectly valid and reliable. Finally, it is always possible that research has been influenced by unintentional biases. These biases can take an infinite variety of forms, such as unintentionally testing the control group in a noisier environment than the one used for testing the experimental group, or a research assistant unintentionally suggesting answers to respondents (without the researcher's knowledge) in an opinion survey. Thus, researchers should not naively set out looking for "proof" by using empirical research methods. Instead, they should recognize that they will be collecting data that offer varying degrees of confidence regarding various conclusions. The greater the degree of care taken in reducing errors, the more confidence in the results researchers are justified in having.

➢ Guideline 2.14 Avoid using two different terms to refer to the same variable in a hypothesis.

In Example 2.14.1, it is not clear whether the "literature-based approach" is the same as the "new approach" because two different terms are being used. This problem has been corrected in the improved version.

Example 2.14.1

Students who receive a literature-based approach to reading instruction plus training in phonetics have better attitudes toward reading than those who receive only the new approach to reading instruction.

Improved Version of Example 2.14.1

Students who receive a literature-based approach to reading instruction plus training in phonetics have better attitudes toward reading than those who receive only the literature-based approach to reading instruction.

Note that clarity of communication is of utmost importance in scientific writing. Varying the terms used to refer to a single construct, as one might do in creative writing, is likely to impede clear scientific communication.

➢ Guideline 2.15 Avoid making precise statistical predictions in a hypothesis.

Precise statistical predictions are rarely justified. In addition, they may make it almost impossible to confirm a hypothesis. Consider Example 2.15.1. If contamination is reduced by any percentage other than 35, the hypothesis would have to be rejected. For instance, if there is a 99% reduction in bacterial contamination, the hypothesis would need to be rejected because it is more than 35%. Likewise, if there is a 1% reduction, the hypothesis would also need to be rejected because it is less than 35%. The improved version indicates the direction of the expected relationship without naming a precise statistical outcome.

Example 2.15.1

The air of operating rooms in which the staff wears polypropylene coveralls contains 35% less bacterial contamination than in the air of operating rooms in which the staff wears conventional surgical clothing.

Improved Version of Example 2.15.1

The air of operating rooms in which the staff wears polypropylene coveralls contains less bacterial contamination than in the air of operating rooms in which the staff wears conventional surgical clothing.

Exercise for Chapter 2

Because the application of many of the guidelines in this chapter involves a certain amount of subjectivity, there may be some legitimate differences of opinions on the best answers to some of the following questions.

PART A: Name the two variables in each of the following hypotheses.

1. There is an inverse relationship between ability to read and frequency of voting among elderly citizens.

2. Among college graduates, authoritarianism and anxiety are directly related.

3. Homeless women are subjected to more spousal physical abuse than are housed women.

4. Mass body index and coronary risk are inversely related among women over 50 years of age.

5. Among first graders, there is a direct relationship between level of hand–eye coordination and achievement in volleyball.

6. Among adolescents, interest in recreational reading is inversely associated with amount of time spent watching television.

PART B: For each of the following hypotheses, identify the independent variable and the dependent variable. (See pages 7–9 to review these terms.)

7. Negative political advertisements are more likely to motivate citizens to vote in general elections than are positive advertisements.

8. Disruptive children who are given token rewards for remaining in their seats in a classroom setting exhibit more in-seat behavior than disruptive children who are given verbal praise.

9. Postcardiac adults who receive telephone counseling to encourage engaging in physical exercise report walking more miles per day than postcardiac adults who do not receive telephone counseling.

PART C: For each of the following hypotheses, name the guideline(s), if any, that were not followed. Revise each hypothesis that you think is faulty. In your revisions, you may need to make some assumptions about what the authors had in mind when writing the hypotheses.

10. The hypothesis is to prove that first-born boys are more athletically competitive than are second-born boys.

11. Children differ in age, and they also differ in their ability to focus on instructional presentations.

12. The rate of development of speech in young children is directly related to the verbal fluency of their parents.

13. Among high achievers, there will be a higher level of sibling rivalry.

14. An individual who experiences marital dissatisfaction tends to be more depressed than an individual who experiences marital satisfaction.

15. Other things being equal, more rewards result in better performance.

16. The social agenda of the present administration is weak.

17. There is a direct relationship between a mechanical engineer's ability to visualize objects rotating in space and his success on the job.

18. Fifty percent of employees with poor attendance records have alcohol-related syndromes.

19. College applicants who take test preparation courses exhibit less test-taking anxiety.

20. First graders whose parents read to them on a regular basis have greater reading achievement.

21. Students who take Psychology 101 report less self-insight on a questionnaire given at the beginning of the course than on a posttest given at the end of an Introduction to Psychology course.

22. People who cheat the welfare system are disreputable.

23. There will be a 25% reduction in the incidence of smoking after high school students complete a unit on the harmful effects of tobacco.

24. Using discussion groups in college sociology classes will be more effective than a traditional lecture approach to instruction.

PART D: Write a simple hypothesis on a topic of interest to you that includes an independent and a dependent variable. Then name the variables in the spaces provided.

Your hypothesis:

Independent variable:

Dependent variable:

PART E: Write a simple hypothesis on a topic of interest to you that does not have independent and dependent variables. Mention a population in the hypothesis.

Your hypothesis:

Chapter 3
A Closer Look at Hypotheses

This chapter presents some advanced guidelines for writing hypotheses and explores some of the principles from Chapter 2 in greater detail.

➢ **Guideline 3.1   A single sentence may contain more than one hypothesis.**

It is permissible to include more than one hypothesis in a single sentence as long as the sentence is reasonably concise and its meaning is clear.

In Example 3.1.1, there is one independent variable ("supplementary group therapy") and two anticipated outcomes or dependent variables. Therefore, there are two hypotheses: (1) Those who receive the group therapy supplement report more relief and (2) Those who receive the group therapy supplement are more satisfied with the counseling process.

Example 3.1.1

Depressed clients whose individual counseling is supplemented with group therapy report more relief from their symptoms and greater satisfaction with the counseling process than comparable clients who receive only individual counseling.

➢ **Guideline 3.2   When a number of related hypotheses are to be stated, consider presenting them in a numbered or lettered list.**

Example 3.2.1 shows a list of three related hypotheses.

Example 3.2.1

It was hypothesized that adolescent high school students' desire to learn academic subjects is more greatly influenced by
1. same-gender peers than opposite-gender peers,
2. peers who are elected to student-body positions than those who have not been elected, and
3. peers who have excelled in nonacademic areas such as sports than those who have not excelled.

A numbered list such as the one in Example 3.2.1 may be helpful when writing other sections of the research report. For instance, when discussing research results, researchers can make statements such as the ones shown in Examples 3.2.2 and 3.2.3. Notice that numbering the hypotheses early in a research report makes it easier to refer clearly to a specific hypothesis without having to restate the entire hypothesis. In Example 3.2.2, this was done with a parenthetical phrase. In Example 3.2.3, there is no parenthetical phrase. Either form is correct. However, many copy editors discourage the overuse of parentheses.

Example 3.2.2

Regarding the first hypothesis (same- versus opposite-gender influence), the results are clear. The mean score for the….

Example 3.2.3

Regarding the influence of same- versus opposite-gender peers specified in Hypothesis Number 1, the results are clear. The mean score for the….

➢ Guideline 3.3   The hypothesis or hypotheses should be stated before the Method section.

The Method section of a research report describes how the researcher tested the hypothesis. Therefore, the hypothesis should be stated before describing the methods used to test the hypothesis.

In journal articles, hypotheses are usually stated in the final paragraphs of the literature review, which serves as an introduction in the research report. Immediately following the literature review is the Method section. (See Example 1.4.1 in Chapter 1 to review the structure of a basic research report.)

In theses and dissertations, the hypotheses are usually stated at the end of the first chapter, which is the introduction. (In a thesis or dissertation, the first chapter is usually the introduction, while the second chapter is the literature review.) The hypotheses may be stated again at the end of the second chapter because the hypotheses should flow logically from the literature that has been reviewed.

➢ Guideline 3.4   While some researchers use alternative terms, the term *hypothesis* is preferred.

Some researchers begin the statements of their hypotheses with terms such as *predicted*, *speculated*, and *expected* in phrases such as the one in Example 3.4.1. While this is acceptable, it is best to use the formal term *hypothesis* or *hypothesized* instead of alternative terms. This is illustrated in Example 3.4.1 and its improved version.

Example 3.4.1

Based on prior research, it was expected that low-income women who are subjected to domestic abuse are at greater risk for being unemployed than low-income women who are not subjected to domestic abuse.

Improved Version of Example 3.4.1

Based on prior research, it was hypothesized that low-income women who are subjected to domestic abuse are at greater risk for being unemployed than low-income women who are not subjected to domestic abuse.

➢ Guideline 3.5 In a research report, a hypothesis should flow from the narrative that immediately precedes it.

A research report typically begins with a literature review, which serves as the introduction to the report. Typically, the hypothesis is stated at the end of the literature review.

There should be a clear, logical connection between the findings in the literature and the researcher's hypothesis. In Example 3.5.1, the researcher explicitly reminds readers of the main thrust of the findings in the literature in order to show readers that the hypothesis flows from the literature (i.e., is logically based on the findings in the literature).

Example 3.5.1

The preceding literature review clearly indicates that teachers in the Salilii tribe rely more heavily on physical punishment than on rewards for maintaining discipline among children in the classroom. The literature also indicates a large number of cultural parallels between the Salilii tribe and the Lani tribe. Thus, it was hypothesized that teachers in the Lani tribe also rely more heavily on physical punishment than on rewards for maintaining discipline.

➢ Guideline 3.6 Both directional and nondirectional hypotheses are acceptable.

Up to this point in this book, all the hypotheses have been directional. A *directional* hypothesis indicates the direction of the difference expected. For instance, in Example 3.6.1, the direction of the difference is clearly stated (i.e., low SES is associated with more authoritarianism). In contrast, Example 3.6.2 is *nondirectional* because it predicts that a difference will be found but does not indicate the direction of the difference.

Example 3.6.1

Directional hypothesis: It is hypothesized that police officers reared in low-socioeconomic-status (SES) families are more authoritarian than police officers reared in middle SES families.

Example 3.6.2

Nondirectional hypothesis: Police officers reared in low-socioeconomic-status families differ in their level of authoritarianism from police officers reared in middle-socioeconomic-status families.

Example 3.6.3 shows a directional hypothesis for an experimental study (i.e., a study in which treatments will be administered in order to see if they cause changes in the participants). It predicts that one group will report a lower level of pain than the other. In contrast, Example 3.6.4 shows a corresponding nondirectional hypothesis, which predicts only that the two groups will differ in their reports of pain. It does not predict which group will report less pain.

Example 3.6.3

Directional hypothesis: It is hypothesized that adult males with Condition X who are administered Drug A report a lower level of pain than a comparable group of males who are administered Drug B.

Example 3.6.4

Nondirectional hypothesis: It is hypothesized that adult males with Condition X who are administered Drug A report a different level of pain than a comparable group of males who are administered Drug B.

When researchers have a basis for predicting the outcome of a study, they should state a directional hypothesis. When they do not have such a basis, they should state a nondirectional one.

Note that directional hypotheses are much more frequently used as the basis for research than nondirectional hypotheses. This is probably true because it is the expectation of specific kinds of differences that usually motivates researchers to conduct research.

➢ Guideline 3.7 When a researcher has a research hypothesis, it should be stated; the null hypothesis need not always be stated.

A *research hypothesis* is the hypothesis that a researcher believes will be supported by his or her data. When a researcher has such a hypothesis (whether it is directional or nondirectional; see the previous guideline), it should be stated in the research report.

In contrast, the *null hypothesis* is a statistical hypothesis that states that a difference is attributable to random errors created by random sampling. For instance, if a random sample is designated as an experimental group and is administered a new drug while another random sample is selected to be the control group, a difference at the end of the experiment might be attributable to inequalities between the two groups created by the random selection (e.g., quite at random, one group might be more predisposed to improve than the other).

In other words, the null hypothesis states that there is no true difference—only a random one. Significance tests are used to test the null hypothesis. (Students who have not taken a statistics course should consult Appendix C for an introduction to the null hypothesis and significance testing.)

In journal articles, formal statements of null hypotheses are almost always omitted because they always have the same content—regardless of how they are worded (i.e., they always attribute any differences to random errors). Thus, it would be redundant to repeat the null hypothesis in all quantitative research reports.

In term projects, theses, and dissertations, however, students are sometimes required to state null hypotheses in order to demonstrate that they understand the purpose of the significance tests they have conducted. (The purpose of a significance test is to test the null hypothesis.) Examples 3.7.1 and 3.7.2 illustrate some ways the null hypothesis can be stated. Because there is more than one way to word a null hypothesis, two statements are shown in each example. Only one statement, however, should be used in a research report.

Example 3.7.1

Research hypothesis: The research hypothesis is that social standing in campus organizations is directly related to gregariousness.

One version of the corresponding null hypothesis: The null hypothesis is that there is no true relationship between social standing in campus organizations and gregariousness.

Another version of the corresponding null hypothesis: The null hypothesis is that the relationship between social standing in campus organizations and gregariousness is nonexistent in the population from which the sample was drawn.

Example 3.7.2

Research hypothesis: The research hypothesis is that private school graduates have a higher proportion of fathers in high-status occupations than public school graduates.

One version of the corresponding null hypothesis: The null hypothesis is that there is no true difference in the proportion of fathers in high-status occupations between the populations of private school and public school graduates.

Another version of the corresponding null hypothesis: The null hypothesis is that the observed difference between the proportions of fathers in high-status occupations for private school graduates and public school graduates is the result of chance variations associated with the random sampling process.

Exercise for Chapter 3

Because the application of many of the guidelines in this chapter involves a certain amount of subjectivity, there may be some legitimate differences of opinions on the best answers to some of the questions.

PART A: Answer the questions based on the guidelines presented in this chapter.

1. Is it permissible to include more than one hypothesis in a single sentence? Explain.

2. Very briefly explain why it may be helpful to present a numbered (or lettered) list of hypotheses when more than one hypothesis will be examined in a single research study.

3. In journal articles, where are hypotheses usually stated?

4. In theses and dissertations, where are hypotheses usually stated?

5. According to this chapter, how could the following statement be improved?

   "Based on the literature reviewed above, it was predicted that politicians who emphasize position XXX are viewed more favorably by the electorate than politicians who emphasize position YYY."

6. Rewrite the following directional hypothesis to make it nondirectional.

   "Primary-grade students taught reading with the XYZ method obtain higher reading comprehension test scores than those taught with the ABC method."

7. Write a null hypothesis that corresponds to the following research hypothesis.

   "It is hypothesized that there is a direct relationship between the extent to which social workers empathize with their clients and the clients' rate of compliance with the XYZ rule."

PART B

8. Write a directional hypothesis on a topic of interest to you. Then write a corresponding null hypothesis for it.

9. Rewrite the directional hypothesis that you wrote for Question 8 to make it nondirectional.

PART C

10. If you will be writing a thesis or dissertation, examine theses or dissertations in your college/university library. Do any of them contain statements of the null hypothesis? If yes, copy one, and bring it to class for discussion.

Notes

Chapter 4
Writing Research
Objectives and Questions

The previous two chapters cover writing research hypotheses, which indicate the predicted relationship among two or more variables.[1] This chapter covers two alternatives to hypotheses: research objectives (also called research purposes) and research questions.

➢ Guideline 4.1   When no relationship will be examined, consider stating a research objective.

In Example 4.1.1, no relationships are being examined. Instead, the researchers want to determine only one thing—the "level of public support." Hence, it would be inappropriate to try to state it as a hypothesis. A statement of the objective is appropriate.

Example 4.1.1

The research objective was to determine the level of public support for the bond issue for funding the construction of additional public libraries.[2]

Likewise, no relationship is implied in Example 4.1.2. Instead, the researchers want to determine only what is being done to provide "practical training on ethical issues...."

Example 4.1.2

The objective of our research was to determine what traditional graduate training programs in nursing were doing to provide practical training on ethical issues regarding euthanasia.

➢ Guideline 4.2   When no relationship will be examined, consider posing a research question.

An alternative to a research objective is a research question. Examples 4.2.1 and 4.2.2 show research objectives restated as research questions.

---

[1] A relationship can take two forms: (a) an *association*, such as higher levels of depression are associated with lower levels of self-esteem and (b) a *difference*, such as those who receive group counseling will be less depressed than those who receive individual counseling.

[2] For a research *proposal*, use the present tense (e.g., "The research objective *is* to determine...").

Example 4.2.1

The research *objective* was to determine the level of public support for the bond issue for funding the construction of additional public libraries.

The research *question* was as follows: What is the level of public support for the bond issue for funding the construction of additional public libraries?

Example 4.2.2

The *objective* of our research was to determine what traditional graduate training programs in nursing were doing to provide practical training on ethical issues regarding euthanasia.

The research *question* was as follows: What are traditional graduate training programs in nursing doing to provide practical training on ethical issues regarding euthanasia?

➤ Guideline 4.3   Stating a research objective or posing a research question are equally acceptable.

The choice between stating a research objective or a research question is a matter of choosing the form that reads more smoothly in a particular context. One form is not inherently preferable to the other.

➤ Guideline 4.4   Avoid writing a research question that implies that the answer will be a simple "yes" or "no."

Example 4.4.1 violates this guideline. Most research is based on complex concepts, and the results are usually not simple. Yet Example 4.4.1 implies that the researchers are interested only in a "yes" or "no" answer. The improved version poses a more realistic question.

Example 4.4.1

Research Question: Do adolescents believe that their peers have favorable views of marijuana?

Improved Version of Example 4.4.1

Research Question: To what extent do adolescents believe that their peers have favorable views of marijuana?

Compare Example 4.4.2 and its improved version. Research on complex human behavior such as reading achievement seldom yields a simple "yes" or "no" answer. Hence, the improved version is superior.

Example 4.4.2

Research Question: In the long run, does a literature-based approach produce higher levels of overall reading achievement than a phonics-based approach?

Improved Version of Example 4.4.2

Research Question: In the long run, what are the relative contributions of literature-based and phonics-based approaches to overall reading achievement?

Of course, the terms "long run," "literature-based [approach]", and "phonics-based [approach]" will need to be defined in the research report. Writing definitions in research is covered in Chapter 7.

➢ Guideline 4.5   When previous research is contradictory, consider using a research objective or a research question instead of a hypothesis.

Sometimes researchers are unwilling to make a prediction because the previous research on the topic has had contradictory findings. Such contradictions can occur for a variety of reasons, such as different researchers using different types of samples and measures in various studies as well as using different definitions of the variables studied. In such a situation, it may be more appropriate to state a research objective or question instead of a hypothesis.

➢ Guideline 4.6   When a new topic is to be examined, consider using a research objective or a research question instead of a hypothesis.

Researchers sometimes identify new problems for research. For instance, prior to the terrorist attacks of September 11, 2001, there had been no research on the psychological effects of terrorism of such great magnitude on children in the United States. In light of the lack of previous research, it may have been more appropriate to state a research question (or objective) instead of a hypothesis, as is done in Example 4.6.1.

Example 4.6.1

Research Question: What was the nature and extent of the psychological impact of the terrorist attack of September 11, 2001, on middle-school children residing in the greater New York City metropolitan area?

Example 4.6.1 could be rewritten as a research objective without changing the meaning of the researcher's question, as illustrated in Example 4.6.2.

Example 4.6.2

Research Objective: To explore the nature and extent of the psychological impact of the terrorist attack of September 11, 2001, on middle-school children residing in the greater New York City metropolitan area.

➤ **Guideline 4.7   For *qualitative* research, consider writing a research objective or question instead of a hypothesis.**

Most qualitative researchers approach their research topics without imposing hypotheses derived from theory or previous research. Instead, they attempt to *follow the data* (i.e., as they analyze the data, they attempt to identify themes and relationships based on participants' responses).

Nevertheless, qualitative researchers need to state one or more research objectives or questions at the onset of their research, even if the objective or question is less specific than the ones posed by quantitative researchers.

Example 4.7.1 shows the research questions for a qualitative study, and Example 4.7.2 shows a research purpose (i.e., research objective). These illustrate the degree of specificity desirable in research questions and objectives for qualitative research. Note that these statements were made in the last paragraph of the literature review, which serves as the introduction to the research. This is the same position in which quantitative researchers state their hypotheses, questions, and objectives.

Example 4.7.1

Thus, the current study utilized a semistructured interview in order to explore how fourth- through eighth-grade teachers perceive and deal with real-life teasing incidents in schools. The following research questions were posed: (a) How do teachers differentiate between teasing and bullying incidents at school? and (b) How do teachers report intervening with teasing incidents at school?[3]

Example 4.7.2

The purpose [i.e., objective] of this study is to examine perceptions held by recipients of adult day services about how intergenerational programming impacted them physically.[4]

➤ **Guideline 4.8   A research objective or question should be as specific as possible, yet be comprehensible.**

The need for specificity in hypotheses is discussed under Guideline 2.5 in Chapter 2. Application of this guideline is often problematic. Consider, for instance, Example 4.8.1. It is quite specific, actually naming two specific instruments (i.e., measuring tools). However, for readers who are not familiar with the specific instruments (e.g., the scale and the inventory), the research objective may be too specific.[5] Thus, writers must judge whether their audi-

---

[3] Smith et al. (2010, p. 7).
[4] Weintraub & Killian (2009, pp. 355–356).
[5] Instruments such as attitude scales and inventories need to be described in detail in the section of the research report on methods. This topic is covered in Chapter 9.

ences are likely to be familiar with the specific item(s) mentioned—in this case, the specific instruments.

For readers who are not familiar with the specific scale and inventory in Example 4.8.1, the improved version is superior. Of course, readers of the research report will expect to learn later in the report how the two variables were measured.

Example 4.8.1

The objective was to determine the extent to which college students' scores on the Voloskovoy Self-Esteem Scale correlate with scores on the Smith-Doe Cultural Tolerance Inventory.

Improved Version of Example 4.8.1

The objective was to determine the extent to which college students' self-esteem correlates with their tolerance of cultural differences.

➢ Guideline 4.9 When stating related objectives or questions, consider presenting them in a numbered or lettered list.

In Example 4.9.1, the researchers present a numbered list of questions.

Example 4.9.1

1. Net of other factors, are Asian students more likely than Latino students to have favorable attitudes toward the quality of school officials?
2. Net of other factors, does generational status significantly affect perceptions of the competency of school officials among immigrant students collectively and Latino and Asian students separately?
3. Net of other factors, does language proficiency significantly affect perceptions of the competency of school officials among immigrant students collectively and Latino and Asian students separately?[6]

The numbered list in Example 4.9.1 allows the researchers to refer to individual research questions by number later in the report. For instance, in the Results section, a researcher might say, "The results for research question number 1 clearly indicate that…" and later make a statement such as "For research question number 2, the results suggest that…."

In Example 4.9.2, the researchers start with a general, overarching research question followed by a lettered list of the specific questions on which data were collected. This arrangement is usually desirable when there are a number of related research questions that were investigated.

---

[6] Watkins & Melde (2010, pp. 10–11).

Example 4.9.2

This study examined the following general research question: How do nurses who leave the nursing profession before retirement age arrive at their decision to leave? The more specific research questions included (a) With whom did they discuss their impending decision? (b) What resources did they consult? (c) How long did they consider the impending decision before finalizing it? and (d) How did they carry out their decision?

➤ Guideline 4.10   A research objective or question should flow from the literature review that immediately precedes it.

Research reports typically begin with a literature review, which serves as the introduction to the report. The literature review should logically lead readers to the research objectives or questions (or hypotheses)—that is, the rationale for formulating the objectives or questions should be made clear by the literature review.

Example 4.10.1 shows the final two sentences of the last paragraph of a literature review on self-cutting (an increasingly frequent form of self-mutilation, especially among adolescents). The research questions that follow the paragraph flow directly from it.

Example 4.10.1

Nevertheless, up to now, there has been no research in Hong Kong to study the self-cutting behavior of adolescents, especially the parental influence and response (Yip, 1998).... We conducted a qualitative study of parental influence on and response to adolescent self-cutting in Hong Kong.

Research Questions
    There were three research questions in this study:
    1. In what ways have the parents influenced their children's self-cutting?
    2. How did the parents respond to their children's self-cutting?
    3. How was the parent–child relationship affected by the self-cutting?[7]

Exercise for Chapter 4

PART A

1. Rewrite this research question as a research objective: "To what extent do primary care physicians and specialists inquire about patients' lifestyle characteristics that may affect patients' overall health?"

---

[7] Yip, Ngan, & Lam (2003, p. 406).

2. Rewrite this research objective as a research question: "The objective of this research is to estimate the extent to which religious affiliation predicts voter sentiment regarding bond issues for public schools."

3. According to this chapter, is stating a research question inherently better than stating a research objective?

4. Which of the guidelines in this chapter is clearly violated in the following research question?

"Is the Internet useful for teaching geography?"

5. "When previous research is contradictory, stating a research hypothesis rather than an objective or question is clearly preferable." Is this statement true *or* false?

6. For which of the following types of research would stating a research hypothesis be less likely?

A. Qualitative research.   B. Quantitative research.

7. Which of the guidelines in this chapter is violated by the following research objective?

"The objective is to determine whether the use of the Barnes Advocacy Teaching Method results in higher scores on the Dobrowsky Scale of International Understanding."

8. Which of the following arrangements is recommended in this chapter?

A. Present a literature review that flows from the research objective or question that is stated first.
B. Present a research objective or question that flows from the literature review that immediately precedes it.

PART B

9. Write a research objective on a topic of interest to you. Then rewrite it as a research question. Which form (objective or question) do you prefer? Why?

PART C

10. Review three journal articles, theses, or dissertations that contain statements of objectives or questions, and make note of the following:

   A. In how many cases are the objectives or questions presented in the last paragraph before the section on methods (i.e., at the end of the literature review)?

   B. In articles that contain more than one objective or question, are the objectives or questions in a numbered (or lettered) list?

Chapter 5
Writing Titles

Because titles perform the important function of helping consumers of research identify research reports that are of interest to them, titles should be written with considerable care.

➢ **Guideline 5.1 If only a small number of variables is studied, the title should name the variables.**

In Example 5.1.1, there are two variables: (1) self-esteem and (2) aggressiveness.

Example 5.1.1

The Relationship Between Self-Esteem and Aggressiveness

In Example 5.1.2, there is one variable: attitudes toward tobacco consumption.

Example 5.1.2

Adolescents' Attitudes Toward Tobacco Consumption

➢ **Guideline 5.2 A title should not be a complete sentence.**

Notice that Examples 5.1.1 and 5.1.2 are not sentences and do not end with a period, both of which are appropriate characteristics of titles.

➢ **Guideline 5.3 If many variables are studied, only the *types* of variables should be named.**

Suppose a researcher examined how students' attitudes toward school change over time with attention to differences among urban, suburban, and rural groups; various socioeconomic groups; girls and boys; and so on. Because there are too many variables to name in a concise title, only the main variable(s) should be specifically named, while the others may be referred to by type, as illustrated in Example 5.3.1. In this example, the main variable of "attitudes toward school" is mentioned, while the term "demographic variables" is used to stand for a variety of background variables such as socioeconomic status and gender.

Example 5.3.1

Relationships Between Students' Attitudes Toward School and Selected Demographic Variables

➢ **Guideline 5.4   The title of a journal article should be concise; the title of a thesis or dissertation may be longer.**

Titles of journal articles tend to be concise. A simple survey that we conducted illustrates this point. A count of the number of words in the titles of a random sample of 152 research articles on mathematics education that appeared in 42 journals in a recent year revealed that the median (average) number of words was close to 11. Example 5.4.1 is the shortest one identified in the survey. It is exceptionally short and could be improved by incorporating a reference to the variables studied.

Example 5.4.1

The Mathematics Department

Example 5.4.2 is the longest title identified in the survey. It is long only because the specific countries are listed. If it ended with "in Various Countries" instead of with the list, it would be more concise but less descriptive. If the research report was for dissemination in the United States, an alternative would be to end the title with "…in the United States and Other Countries."

Example 5.4.2

Grade Placement of Addition and Subtraction Topics in Japan, Mainland China, the Soviet Union, Taiwan, and the United States

Example 5.4.3 shows a title of about average length for the sample of titles examined. It illustrates Guideline 5.4 because the types of variables, "personality factors" and "biographical factors," are referred to, while the specific personality traits and types of biographical data collected are not specifically named.

Example 5.4.3

Contributions of Some Personality and Biographical Factors to Mathematical Creativity

For a random sample of titles of dissertations on mathematics education during the same recent year, the average number of words in the titles was almost 19, which is considerably more than the average of 11 for journal articles. A variation on the longest dissertation title is shown in Example 5.4.4.

Example 5.4.4

A Descriptive Study of Verbal Problems in Mathematics Textbooks for Grades Seven and Eight From Four Decades: the 1970s, the 1980s, the 1990s, and the 2000s

Students who are preparing theses or dissertations should ask their committees whether concise titles—such as those commonly used in journals—or longer titles—which are more typical (but not universal) in theses and dissertations—are expected. If a shorter title is desired, the shortened version shown immediately below illustrates how this could be done.

Shortened Version of the Title in Example 5.4.4

Verbal Problems in Mathematics Textbooks for Grades Seven and Eight for Four Decades From 1970 Through 2010

➢ Guideline 5.5   A title should indicate what was studied—not the findings of the study.

All the previous examples illustrate this guideline. Example 5.5.1 violates the guideline because it states the finding that "practices are associated." This is corrected in the improved version by omitting the result. Also, note that the original version is a complete sentence, which violates Guideline 5.2.

Example 5.5.1

Strong Religious Beliefs and Taking Part in Religious Practices Are Associated With Less Frequent Underage Alcohol Use

Improved Version of Example 5.5.1

The Role of Religious Beliefs and Behaviors in Predicting Underage Alcohol Use[1]

Guideline 5.5 may surprise some beginning students of empirical methods because results and conclusions are often stated in titles in the popular press. This is the case because the press frequently reports straightforward facts. "Five Die in Downtown Hotel Fire" is a perfectly acceptable title for a factual article of limited scope. Because empirical research reports are likely to raise as many questions as they resolve, a title that states a simple factual result or conclusion is usually inappropriate.

---

[1] Brechting, et al. (2010, p. 324).

➢ Guideline 5.6 Consider mentioning the population(s) in a title.

This guideline is especially applicable when a study has been deliberately delimited to a particular population. In Example 5.6.1, the population is delimited to Hawaiian youth in rural communities.

Example 5.6.1

Exploring Culturally Specific Drug Resistance Strategies of Hawaiian Youth in Rural Communities[2]

In Example 5.6.2, the title indicates that the population consists of older Asian adults. Such information helps consumers of research identify articles on populations of interest to them.

Example 5.6.2

Hand Dominance and Grip Strength of Older Asian Adults[3]

Note that sometimes a particular type of participant is studied only because that type is readily available to a researcher. For instance, a researcher might conduct a study on a theory of learning using students enrolled in his or her introductory psychology class (because they are readily available) even though the researcher is interested in the application of the theory to students in general. In such a case, mention of the type of population in the title is less important than when a researcher deliberately selects participants from a particular population of special interest.

➢ Guideline 5.7 Consider the use of subtitles to indicate the methods of study.

While it is not necessary to mention the methods used to conduct a study (e.g., a survey, an experiment, and so on), this information can be helpful for consumers of research trying to identify particular types of studies. However, when initially trying to locate research reports on a given topic, most consumers are more interested in the variables studied (and the populations) than in the method(s) used to conduct the studies. This suggests that it is best to name variables and populations in the main title, followed by a subtitle indicating the method used to conduct the study. This is illustrated in the improved versions of Examples 5.7.1 and 5.7.2.

Example 5.7.1

A Pilot Study on the Role of Alcoholism in Dysfunctional Families

---

[2] Okamoto, Poʻa-Kekuawela, Chin, Nebre, & Helm (2010, p. 56).
[3] Wang (2010, p. 897).

Improved Version of Example 5.7.1

The Role of Alcoholism in Dysfunctional Families: A Pilot Study

Example 5.7.2

A National Survey of Experienced Kindergarten Teachers' Definitions of Literacy

Improved Version of Example 5.7.2

Experienced Kindergarten Teachers' Definitions of Literacy: A National Survey

➢ Guideline 5.8   If a study is strongly tied to a particular model or theory, consider mentioning it in the title.

Some consumers of research are especially interested in studies that shed light on particular models or theories. If a study was designed to explore some aspect of these, mentioning this in the title will help consumers locate relevant research. In Example 5.8.1, a theory is mentioned in the subtitle, while a theory is mentioned in the main title of Example 5.8.2. While either placement is acceptable, note that Example 5.8.2 places more emphasis on the theory than does Example 5.8.1.

Example 5.8.1

The Role of Male Siblings in the Mathematics Achievement of Adolescent Girls: A Social Learning Theory Perspective

Example 5.8.2

Application of the Theory of Planned Behavior in the Treatment of Adolescents With Multi-Drug Dependence Issues

➢ Guideline 5.9   Omit the names of specific measures unless they are the focus of the research.

Mentioning specific measures in titles can make them unnecessarily long without providing key information to consumers of research. Example 5.9.1 shows a title that has been made unnecessarily long by naming a specific instrument. Compare it with the improved version.

Example 5.9.1

The Effectiveness of a Home Care Program for Improving the Functional Abilities of Elderly Individuals as Measured by the Functional Abilities Self-Rating Scale

Improved Version of Example 5.9.1

The Effectiveness of a Home Care Program for Improving the Functional Abilities of Elderly Individuals

The main exception to this guideline is when the instruments are the focus of the research, such as research on the reliability and validity of specific instruments. Example 5.9.2 shows a title in which it is appropriate to name a specific instrument.

Example 5.9.2

Development of the Grandparents' Role Identity Scale: A Reliability and Validity Study

➢ **Guideline 5.10 A title may be in the form of a question, but this form should be used sparingly and with caution.**

Questions, when used as titles, are less formal than titles expressed in the form of statements. Thus, questions as titles are sometimes preferred in less formal types of publications such as staff newsletters and workshop materials.

When using a question as a title for a research report, avoid stating it as a question that implies that it can be answered with a simple "yes" or "no." Notice that the title in Example 5.10.1 implies that the result will be a simple "yes" or "no" answer, which is seldom the case in empirical research because empirical methods yield varying degrees of confidence in results—not final answers. In the first improved version of Example 5.10.1, the problem has been fixed by posing the question in such a way that it cannot be answered with a simple "yes" or "no." The second improved version of Example 5.10.1 shows that the problem can be avoided by using a statement instead of a question.

Example 5.10.1

Do Private Colleges and Universities Accommodate Students With Physical Disabilities?

First Improved Version of Example 5.10.1

To What Extent Do Private Colleges and Universities Accommodate Students With Physical Disabilities?

Second Improved Version of Example 5.10.1

Private College and Universities' Accommodations of Students With Physical Disabilities

➢ **Guideline 5.11 In titles, use the words *effect* and *influence* with caution.**

The words *effect* and *influence* are frequently used in the titles of research reports in which cause-and-effect relationships were studied. To examine such relationships, true experimental, quasi-experimental, or rigorous ex post facto methods should usually be employed. As a general rule, only reports on these methods should contain these words in their titles.

Examples 5.11.1 and 5.11.2 illustrate the appropriate use of the word *effect* in titles of reports on experiments. The typical form is as follows: "The effect(s) of an independent variable (treatment or stimulus) on a dependent variable (outcome or response)."

Example 5.11.1

The Effects of Three Schedules of Reinforcement on the Maze Performance of Rats

Example 5.11.2

The Effects of Having Students Retell Stories in Writing on Their Achievement on a Standardized Test of Writing Skills

Note that *effects* is used as a noun in the two examples. As a noun, it means "influence." When used as a noun, the word *affect* means "feelings or emotions." Clearly, *effect* is the correct noun to use in these examples.

➢ Guideline 5.12   A title should be consistent with the research hypothesis, objective, purpose, or question.

In Examples 5.12.1 and 5.12.2, research purposes are stated. The corresponding titles closely mirror the statements of purpose.

Example 5.12.1

Research Purpose: The purpose of this study was to assess the value of research from the perspective of alumni who completed an undergraduate research (UGR) project in family and consumer sciences.

Corresponding Title: Perceptions of the Value of Undergraduate Research: A Pilot Qualitative Study of Human Sciences Graduates[4]

Example 5.12.2

Research Purpose: The purpose of this study was to examine the effects of peer mentoring and social skills training on social interactions of three children with a history of child maltreatment.

Corresponding Title: Effects of a Peer Engagement Program on Socially Withdrawn Children With a History of Maltreatment[5]

---

[4] Collins, Hymon-Parker, Mitstifer, & Nelson Goff (2010, p. 303).
[5] Mathews, Fawcett, & Sheldon (2009, pp. 270–272).

➤ **Guideline 5.13   Consider mentioning unique features of a study in its title.**

Suppose a researcher conducted the first long-term follow-up study on the effects of a drug. The researcher would be wise to indicate in the title that the study is a long-term one, as shown in Example 5.13.1.

Example 5.13.1

The Long-Term Effects of Tetracycline on Tooth Enamel Erosion

➤ **Guideline 5.14   Avoid using "clever" titles.**

In Example 5.14.1, only the phrase "Publishing Criminal Justice Research" is informative. The reader will assume that an article deals with contemporary issues unless the title indicates that the study is historical. Thus, reference to the new millennium is not needed. The subtitle is completely uninformative and appears to have been written in an effort to be clever.

Example 5.14.1

Publishing Criminal Justice Research in the New Millennium: Things Gutenberg Never Taught You

In Example 5.14.2, "Taking the Sting Out of Stuttering" is a rhetorical phrase that does not contribute to the readers' understanding of the topic of the research. The phrase should be omitted.

Example 5.14.2

Taking the Sting Out of Stuttering: A Comparison of the Effectiveness of Two Methods for Treating Stuttering

In general, throughout research reports, avoid the temptation to be clever or humorous. The function of a research report is to inform—not to entertain.

➤ **Guideline 5.15   Learn the conventions for capitalization in titles.**

In APA style, titles at the beginning of research reports follow the usual rules of capitalization for titles as illustrated in all the titles in this chapter. However, in a reference list, only three elements are capitalized: (1) the first letter of the first word, (2) the first letter of the first word in a subtitle, and (3) proper nouns. This is illustrated in all the references in the reference list near the end of this book.

Exercise for Chapter 5

PART A

1. When should the types of variables (instead of the individual variables) be mentioned in a title?

2. Do the titles of journal articles tend to be longer than the titles of theses and dissertations?

3. Why should a researcher avoid stating the findings of a study in the title?

4. According to this chapter, which are more formal as titles: "statements" *or* "questions"?

5. Which of the following titles is correct?
   A. The Affects of Treatment A on Outcome B
   B. The Effects of Treatment A on Outcome B

PART B: Comment on the adequacy of each of the following titles for research articles.

6. Child Care Subsidies Increase the Number of Mothers Who Are Employed Full-Time

7. Watering the Proverbial Garden: Effective Communication Between Teachers and School Administrators

8. The Political Scientist

9. Are Age and Tenure Related to the Job Satisfaction of Social Workers?

10. Can Economists Predict Recessions?

11. The Effects of Peer Coaching on Achievement in English, Mathematics, History, Foreign Language, Geography, and Physics Among Tenth-, Eleventh-, and Twelfth-Graders: An Experiment Conducted in Five Major Urban Areas During the 2009–2010 School Year Using Multiple Measures of Achievement With Analyses by Gender and Grade Level

12. Forbidden Fruit Tastes Especially Sweet: A Study of Lawyers' Ethical Behavior

13. The Out-Migration From Southern California Is Driven by High Housing Costs

14. Self-Monitoring by Employees Increases the Productivity of Online Workers

PART C: Write a title that you think would be appropriate for a research report that has this research objective: "The objective of this research was to explore the effects of second-shift work schedules on psychological distress in young blue-collar families."

PART D: Write a research objective or hypothesis on a topic of interest to you, and write an appropriate title.

Chapter 6
Writing Introductions and Literature Reviews

The purpose of an introduction and literature review in an empirical research report is to introduce the problem area, establish its importance, and establish the context for the current study.

The guidelines that follow apply to all types of empirical research reports, except where noted.

> ➤ **Guideline 6.1   In theses and dissertations, the first chapter is usually an introduction.**

The introduction in a thesis or dissertation should start by indicating the problem area and the importance of the problem, followed by a summary of the approach that will be used to investigate the problem. Typically, this chapter concludes with a statement of the research hypotheses, objectives, or questions that underlie the study being reported on.

Usually, there are relatively few references to literature in this chapter because a comprehensive literature review is presented in the second chapter. However, it is acceptable to refer to some highlights of the literature review with statements such as, "As will be shown in the next chapter, most of the surveys on this topic have revealed...."

> ➤ **Guideline 6.2   In theses and dissertations, the second chapter presents a comprehensive literature review.**

Students who are preparing theses and dissertations are typically expected to present comprehensive literature reviews in the second chapter. These reviews are usually much more comprehensive than those in other research reports, such as reports in journals and reports for term projects.

The requirement for a comprehensive literature review stems from the fact that a thesis or dissertation is, in effect, a test (i.e., an extended take-home examination) in which students are to demonstrate their ability to identify all literature of relevance to a topic and to synthesize it (i.e., evaluate and present the literature in a way that helps make sense of the individual pieces).

The research hypotheses, objectives, or questions might be restated at the end of the literature review chapter.

➤ Guideline 6.3   In most research reports, literature reviews serve as the introduction to the reports.

In reports, such as those in journals and those prepared for term projects, the literature review typically is used to introduce the topic of the research. In other words, instead of starting with an introduction that presents the writers' personal views on the problem, writers cite literature to introduce the problem.

Example 6.3.1 shows the first paragraph of a literature review in which the topic of driving under the influence (DUI) programs is introduced with citations to literature on the topic.

Example 6.3.1

Clients who present to driving under the influence (DUI) programs come with a variety of problems and situations and the DUI counselor must be able to adapt his or her work to the individual client's needs (Cavaiola & Wuth, 2002; Lapham et al., 2001; Wieczorek & Nochajski, 2005). Most have some sort of problem with alcohol; a meta-analysis study of first-offense and multiple-offense DUI clients found that rates of alcohol use disorders in this population could range from 4% to 92%, depending on the instruments used or how assessments were made (Stasiewicz, Nochajski, & Homish, 2007). Another study of multiple-offense DUI clients found 100% with a lifetime alcohol use disorder and 71% with a lifetime drug use disorder (Lapham, C'de Baca, McMillan, & Lapidus, 2006). Multiple offenders, when compared to first offenders, have been found to be more open and receptive to changing their drinking (Wieczorek & Nochajski, 2005).[1]

➤ Guideline 6.4   In most research reports, literature reviews are selective.

In reports other than theses and dissertations, literature reviews are selective, including references only to the most relevant literature. The literature review needs to be only long enough to bring the reader up-to-date regarding current thinking on and knowledge of a problem and to establish the context for the current research.

➤ Guideline 6.5   A literature review should be an essay—not a list of annotations.

An annotation is a brief summary. A list of annotations indicates what research is available on a topic but fails to organize the material for the reader. Specifically, a list of annotations fails to indicate how the individual citations relate to one another and what trends the writer has observed in the published literature.

---

[1] DiStefano & Hohman, (2010, pp. 180–181).

46

To implement this guideline, it is best to begin by preparing a topic outline such as the one in Example 6.5.1 to guide in writing a literature review. When writing the review based on such an outline, the temptation to string together a set of annotations will be minimized.

Example 6.5.1

Topic Outline for a Literature Review

1. Importance of question-asking by children
   a. As a skill used in learning in school
   b. As a functional skill in the home and other nonschool settings
2. Introduction to two basic types of questions
   a. Request for factual information (who, what, and when)
   b. Questions about causation (why)
   c. Functions of the two types in school
3. Relationship between parents' and children's verbal behavior
   a. On other verbal variables
   b. On question-asking behavior: quantity and type
4. Relationship between culture and verbal behavior
   a. Examples of how and why cultures may vary in their question-asking behavior
   b. Functions of questions in target cultures
5. Statement of the research objectives
   a. Determine types and numbers of questions asked by children in a structured learning environment
   b. Determine the relationship between question-asking by children and by parents, with attention to both number and type
   c. Determine differences in question-asking behavior among target cultures

➢ Guideline 6.6   A literature review should lead logically to research hypotheses, objectives, or questions.

Having read a literature review, readers should understand why the researcher has formulated the specific hypotheses, objectives, or questions that underlie the research being reported. For instance, the current research might be designed to (1) extend the prior research into new areas or with new populations, (2) improve on the prior research in terms of the research methods used, or (3) test some tenet of a theory described in the literature review.

Note that new topics that are unrelated to any existing literature are exceedingly rare. Progress in science is usually based on researchers building on the previous work of other researchers. A literature review should show this progression, especially the progression from the existing literature to the current study.

➤ **Guideline 6.7 Research hypotheses, objectives, or questions should usually be stated at the end of the literature review.**

In light of Guideline 6.6, it is logical to place research hypotheses, objectives, or questions at the end of a literature review.[2] Notice in Example 6.5.1 that the last topic (Topic 5) for the literature review is a statement of the research objectives.

➤ **Guideline 6.8 Research reports with similar findings or methodologies should usually be cited together.**

This guideline is illustrated in Example 6.8.1. Notice that in the example, the information in the first sentence is supported by three references.

Example 6.8.1

The developmental period immediately after high school is characterized by increases in rates of heavy episodic drinking, marijuana use, and cigarette smoking (Arnett, 2005; Bachman et al., 1997; White et al., 2006).[3]

Example 6.8.2 also illustrates this guideline. Notice that three references are cited in a single, cohesive paragraph dealing with one topic.

Example 6.8.2

Contrary to popular belief, most abductors do not use physical force to seize their victims (Finkelhor, Hotaling, & Sedlak, 1990; Poche, Brouwer, & Swearingen, 1981). Instead, they establish rapport with the child, using verbal lures to convince the child to willfully leave with them. In one investigation, an alarming 90% of 3 to 6 year olds who were approached by a stranger left with the stranger after he or she asked them to leave (Poche et al., 1981). Most children do not know an appropriate and effective way to resist enticement from potential abductors.[4]

➤ **Guideline 6.9 The importance of a topic should be explicitly stated.**

It can be a mistake to assume that readers already know the importance of a problem. Even if they are already aware that a problem is of some importance, they may not be aware of its seriousness or all its implications.

Typically, the importance of the topic should be established near the beginning of a literature review. Be specific in giving reasons for the impor-

---

[2] As noted in Guideline 6.1, the research hypotheses, objectives, or questions usually are stated at the end of Chapter 1 (the Introduction) and may be restated at the end of Chapter 2 (the Literature Review) in theses and dissertations; see Guideline 6.2.

[3] Fleming, White, & Catalano (2010, p. 153).

[4] Tarasenko, Miltenberger, Brower-Breitwieser, & Bosch (2010, p. 220).

tance of the topic, as illustrated in Example 6.9.1, which is the beginning of the first paragraph in a literature review.

Example 6.9.1

Obstructive sleep apnea syndrome is characterized by repeated episodes of complete or partial airflow interruptions during sleep, resulting in intermittent hypoxemia associated with brief arousals. Neuropsychological deficits, including memory, attention, motor ability, and executive function impairments, have all been reported for patients with obstructive sleep apnea (Bédard, Montplaisir, Richer, Rouleau, & Malo, 1991....)[5]

Note that nonspecific statements of importance are inappropriate. For instance, the statement in Example 6.9.2 was made in a proposal for a thesis in which a functional skills program in adult schools was to be evaluated. Notice that the statement fails to deal specifically with functional skills in adult education. In fact, the statement is so broad that it could refer to almost any curriculum and instruction topic in education.

Example 6.9.2

Nonspecific statement of importance (not recommended): Human resource is one of the greatest resources of this country, and education plays a major role in maintaining, nurturing, and protecting that resource. Thus, it is imperative that we find, evaluate, and utilize educational systems that yield the results necessary for the country's progress.

➢ Guideline 6.10   Consider pointing out the number or percentage of individuals who are affected by the problem.

Showing that many individuals are affected by a problem helps to establish the importance of a research project. When possible, the specific numbers and percentages should be indicated—not just referred to in the form of nonspecific generalizations such as "A large percentage of high school students report that..." or "An increasing number of individuals have...."

The authors of Example 6.10.1 provide specific percentages.

Example 6.10.1

The Latino population in the United States is rapidly growing, compared to other ethnic groups, and includes a large number of immigrants (U.S. Census Bureau, 2002). Mexican Americans (Mexican heritage persons living in the United States) are the largest and fastest growing Latino subgroup, representing 59.3% of the Latino population and 7.4% of the U.S. population (U.S. Census Bureau, 2001, 2004). Mexican-origin youth face the challenge of adapting to the mainstream

---

[5] Daurat, Huet, & Tiberge (2010, p. 289).

culture while also maintaining ties with and adapting to the Mexican American culture....[6]

In a similar fashion, the authors of Example 6.10.2 established the importance of mentoring interventions by indicating the number of agencies providing the service, with the obvious implication that thousands of individuals are affected.

Example 6.10.2

Mentoring interventions have proliferated in the United States across the past decade, with more than 4,500 agencies now providing this type of service for youth, and government agencies allocating millions of dollars to support them (Dubois & Karcher, 2005; Rhodes, 2002).[7]

Note that Examples 6.10.1 and 6.10.2 were drawn from the first paragraphs of literature reviews. It is common for writers to begin literature reviews by reporting the numbers and percentages of individuals affected by a problem.

➢ Guideline 6.11   Discuss theories that have relevance to the current research.

A *theory* is a cohesive set of principles that helps explain relationships among variables. Pointing out how the research relates to theories helps to establish the context for the research and its importance. Discussion of theories can be integrated throughout the literature review. Typically, the major propositions of a theory and their implications (i.e., what they predict) should be briefly described, as in Example 6.11.1.

Example 6.11.1

Problem behavior theory seeks to explain adolescent drinking behavior from a psychosocial perspective, incorporating the personality, perceived environment, and behavior of the young drinker (Jessor, 1987; Jessor & Jessor, 1977). The behavior system component of problem behavior theory states that youths who engage in one problem behavior, such as alcohol use, are at risk of engaging in other problem behaviors, such as problem drinking, drug use, sexual intercourse, and deviant behaviors. Alcohol use is one part of a syndrome of problem behavior engagement that is linked to negative distal outcomes. Problem behavior theory, specifically the behavior system component, influenced the theoretical framework for this study.[8]

---

[6] Knight et al. (2010, p. 445).
[7] Thomson & Zand (2010, p. 434).
[8] Mancha, Rojas-Neese, & Latimer (2010, p. 211).

Note that being able to show that a research project is theory-based is an important way to justify conducting a study because theory-building is a foundation that helps the scientific community understand the relationships among findings.

➢ Guideline 6.12 Consider commenting on the relevance and importance of the research being cited.

If a study is especially relevant or important, consider mentioning it, as is done in Examples 6.12.1 and 6.12.2.

Example 6.12.1

The most revealing experiment on this topic was conducted by Doe (2010), who used a novel treatment to demonstrate that....

Example 6.12.2

Of most relevance to the current research, the National Synthesis Survey (Smith, 2010) revealed that....

➢ Guideline 6.13 Point out trends in the literature.

In Example 6.13.1, the researchers point out a trend in the findings reported in the research literature.

Example 6.13.1

Numerous studies have indicated that attitudes and behaviors associated with students' work habits and overall diligence are consistently related to higher achievement (e.g., Carbonaro, 2005; Farkas et al., 1990; Olneck & Bills, 1980; Rosenbaum, 2001; Smerdon, 1999).[9]

➢ Guideline 6.14 Point out gaps in the literature.

In Example 6.14.1, the researcher points out gaps in the literature on attitudes toward substance-abuse-treatment clients.

Example 6.14.1

Much has been written about the attitudes of treatment professionals toward substance-abusing clients. Clinical literature and empirical research have suggested that these attitudes are an important element of substance abuse treatment and that they are often somewhat negative (Amodeo, 2000; Amodeo, Fassler, & Griffin, 2002; Googins, 1984; Silverman, 1993; Strozier, 1995; Wechsler & Rohman, 1982). However, a relative gap in the literature exists concerning attitudes toward

---

[9] Covay & Carbonaro (2010, p. 23).

clients who enter substance abuse treatment under the particular condition of being mandated to treatment by the courts.[10]

In Example 6.14.2, the researchers point out a gap in research on self-rated health.

Example 6.14.2

Relatively few studies have examined the effect of excess body weight on self-rated health (Ferraro & Booth, 1999; Ford et al., 2001). This is a crucial gap in the literature because self-rated health is an excellent comprehensive indicator of individual and population health status (Idler & Benyamini, 1997).[11]

Pointing out gaps is especially important when the purpose of the current research is to fill one or more of the gaps.

➢ Guideline 6.15   Be prepared to justify statements regarding gaps in the literature.

Students who are writing term project papers, theses, and dissertations should note that when they point out gaps in the literature, they may be asked by their professors to defend such assertions. Thus, it is a good idea to keep careful records of how the literature search was conducted (i.e., what indices and databases were examined, including the dates) and which descriptors (i.e., subject index terms) were used in the search. Students should consider including a statement such as the one in Example 6.15.1 in their reports.

Example 6.15.1

A search of the ABC Index for the years 1975 through 2010 using the subject index terms "term a" and "term b" yielded only two studies of adolescents (i.e., Doe, 2009; Jones, 2010) and no studies of children.

➢ Guideline 6.16   Point out how the current study differs from previous studies.

It is usually desirable to point out how the current study differs from previous ones. The differences may be in terms of the selection of variables, how the variables were conceptualized and measured, the composition of the sample, the method of analysis, and so on. Example 6.16.1 illustrates how this might be done.

---

[10] Vairo (2010, p. 81).
[11] Zajacova & Burgard (2010, p. 93).

Example 6.16.1

All the studies reported previously relied on self-reports by adolescents as the source of the data. In the current study, reports by the parents of adolescents were used.

➤ Guideline 6.17   Use direct quotations sparingly.

This guideline is suggested for three reasons. First, direct quotations often do not convey their full meaning when quoted out of context. Second, quotations may disrupt the flow of the review because of the varying writing styles of the authors. Finally, quotations sometimes bog down readers in details that are not essential for the purpose of obtaining an overview of the literature. By paraphrasing instead of quoting, minor details can be easily omitted.

Direct quotations are appropriate when the writer of the review (1) wants to illustrate either the original author's skill at writing or lack thereof or (2) believes that the wording of a statement will have an emotional impact on the reader that would be lost in paraphrase. These purposes seldom arise in presenting literature in an empirical research report.

Direct quotations are also appropriate when citing carefully crafted definitions that have been included in previous research reports. Chapter 7 provides guidelines on writing definitions.

➤ Guideline 6.18   Report sparingly on the details of the literature being cited.

Because the research being cited has usually been published, readers can obtain copies to learn the details.

Typically, reviews of literature in theses and dissertations contain more details on cited research than reviews in research reports published as journal articles. Even in theses and dissertations, however, writers should be selective in reporting details. For instance, it may be appropriate to describe an especially relevant and important study in more detail than other studies.

➤ Guideline 6.19   Consider using literature to provide the historical context for the present study.

Following this guideline is especially desirable in theses and dissertations where students should demonstrate that they have a comprehensive knowledge of the literature on their topics. It is also appropriate in research reports published as journal articles when researchers wish to (1) acknowledge the original proponents' theories and principles that underlie their current studies or (2) show that their research is a logical continuation of the historical chain of thought on a topic.

Examples 6.19.1 and 6.19.2 show how the history of a topic might be briefly traced.

Example 6.19.1

Theory and research traditions associated with psychology, and developmental psychology in particular, have been framed in a deficit perspective about youth. G. Stanly Hall (1904) initiated this perspective with his description of adolescence as a time of inevitable storm and stress. Similarly, Anna Freud (1969) viewed adolescence as a period of normative developmental disturbance, and Erik Erikson (1968) believed that youth identity was born of crisis....

Research in the latter decades of the 20th century, however, began to focus on the study of positive youth development. This alternative conception is derived from developmental systems theories (Lerner, 1998), which underscores the potential for plasticity in human development....[12]

Example 6.19.2

Although its origins date back over 100 years (Chapman, 1994), bodybuilding did not move into mainstream culture until the 1960s (Schwarzenegger & Dobbins, 1998). Since then, it has seen a steady rise in popularity. The National Physique Committee (NPC; personal communication, May 17, 2008) estimates their bodybuilding membership to be at 20,000, with an annual increase of 1,000 new members. The International Federation of Body Building (IFBB) estimates that their annual membership also increases by 1,000 members annually (IFBB, personal communication, May 17th, 2008). With its popular movement into American culture, bodybuilding is no longer a fringe activity.[13]

➤ Guideline 6.20   Consider citing prior literature reviews.

Before citing prior literature reviews, examine the literature cited in the reviews to determine if the reviewers have accurately characterized the literature.

When citing prior reviews, summarize their major conclusions, and then bring readers up-to-date by discussing the literature published since the prior reviews were published.

---

[12] Theokas et al. (2005, p. 114).
[13] Parish, Baghurst, & Turner (2010, p. 152).

> ➤ **Guideline 6.21   When using the "author-date method" for citing references, decide whether to emphasize authorship or content.**

Note that in the author-date method for citing references (also known as the Harvard method)[14] only the authors' last names and year of publication are given within the text (with full bibliographic references provided in the reference list at the end).

In the author-date method, names may be made part of the sentence, as in Example 6.21.2. In Example 6.21.1, the emphasis is on the authorship.

Example 6.21.1

Doe (2010) reported that a major source of dissatisfaction among teachers appears to be the low social status accorded their profession.

As an alternative, the names may be included parenthetically, as in Example 6.21.2. By using the parenthetical method, writers emphasize the content of the statement, not its authorship.

Example 6.21.2

A major source of dissatisfaction among teachers appears to be the low social status accorded their profession (Doe, 2010).

Because a literature review should be an essay that integrates and evaluates the content of previous research on a topic, presenting the researcher's name in parentheses, as in Example 6.21.2, is usually preferable because it deemphasizes the authorship.

Of course, sometimes authorship is important and should be emphasized—for instance, when comparing the thoughts of two leading theorists.

> ➤ **Guideline 6.22   Avoid referring to the credentials and affiliations of the researchers.**

In an "appeal to authority," writers in the popular press often refer to a researcher's credentials (e.g., being a professor) and affiliations (e.g., Harvard University) when summarizing research. Thus, in a newspaper article on recently released research, it would not be uncommon to see a statement such as "Professor Doe of Harvard University's School of Public Health reported in an article published today in the *Journal of Studies* that...." Such a statement in a formal academic report of empirical research should almost never be used because scholars' confidence in the results of a research study should

---

[14] This method has been popularized by the *Publication Manual of the American Psychological Association* and is in widespread use throughout the social and behavioral sciences.

rest on the strength of the evidence presented (in light of the care with which empirical methods were used in the research)—not on the credentials or affiliations of the researchers.

> ### ➢ Guideline 6.23 Terminology in a literature review should reflect the tentative nature of empirical data.

Empirical research is inherently subject to error. Despite their best efforts, researchers conduct research with limitations. For instance, samples are often less than ideal, and measures are almost always less than perfectly valid and reliable. As a result, empirical data offer only degrees of evidence. Of course, some evidence is stronger than other evidence, so care should be used in how the evidence is described. As a result, the word *proof* or any of its derivatives (e.g., *proved*) should never be used to describe the results of an empirical study.

For studies that are reasonably strong (e.g., employing adequate samples and reasonable measures), statements such as those in Example 6.23.1 may be used (italics added for emphasis). Note that they are relatively neutral regarding the strength of the evidence.

Example 6.23.1

A recent study *indicates* that....

Two experiments *yielded evidence* that....

Doe (2010) *reported* that....

For studies that are very strong (e.g., employing excellent samples and highly valid and reliable measures), statements such as those in Example 6.23.2 may be used (italics added for emphasis). Note that they indicate that the evidence is strong.

Example 6.23.2

The results of a major national survey *strongly indicate* that....

Taken together, the experiments described above *provide strong evidence* that....

The result of Doe's (2011) seminal research *strongly suggests* that....

For studies that are very weak (e.g., clearly biased samples and measures of highly questionable validity and reliability), statements such as those in Example 6.23.3 may be used (italics added for emphasis). Note that they indicate that the evidence is weak.

Example 6.23.3

In a *preliminary pilot study*, Doe (2010) found that....

In *light of its methodological weaknesses*, the results of this study should be viewed....

While all of the experiments cited above suggest that X is more effective than Y, the failure to use random assignment *seriously limits confidence* in the results.

➤ Guideline 6.24 Avoid using long strings of reference citations for a single finding or theory.

Some findings or theories have been very widely reported in the literature. Suppose, for instance, that there are 32 journal articles that reported data that support the XYZ theory. It would be distracting as well as unproductive to make a simple statement to this effect followed by 32 reference citations in parentheses. One solution is to simply use *e.g.* (which stands for "for example") and cite only a few, as illustrated in Example 6.24.1.

Example 6.24.1

More than 30 experiments reported in journal articles have lent support to the XYZ theory (e.g., Doe, 2009; Jones, 2011; Smith & Smith, 2010).

Another solution is to indicate the time span over which the support has been reported while citing only some of the early and some of the more recent experiments, as in Example 6.24.2.

Example 6.24.2

More than 30 experiments reported in journal articles have lent support to the XYZ theory, starting with studies conducted more than 50 years ago (e.g., Barnes, 1950; Black, 1949;) and continuing to the present (Jones, 2011; Smith & Smith, 2010).

Still another solution is to cite only those that are strongest in terms of research methodology, as in Example 6.24.3.

Example 6.24.3

More than 30 experiments reported in journal articles have lent support to the XYZ theory. Among these, three used true experimental designs with random assignment to treatment groups (Banner & Brown, 2010; Clive, 2011; Tanner, 2008).

Yet another solution is to distinguish among the reports based on the strength of their support, as in Example 6.24.4.

Example 6.24.4

More than 30 experiments reported in journal articles have lent support to the XYZ theory. While the support is weak in about half the studies (e.g., Blake, 2009; Green, 2010), stronger support has been reported in the others (e.g., Shoemaker, 2010; White, 2008).

In a thesis or dissertation, students may be expected to cite all relevant references to demonstrate that a comprehensive literature search has been conducted. Even in this circumstance, long strings of citations can be avoided by referring to the references in smaller groups. For instance, the methodologically stronger ones can be cited in one group while weaker ones can be cited in another. Other examples are (1) citing studies that use one approach (e.g., experiments) in a separate group from those that use a different approach (e.g., surveys), (2) separating older studies from newer studies, and (3) calling special attention to a study that represents a turning point in understanding an issue.

➤ Guideline 6.25 Use of the first person is acceptable if used sparingly.

Use of the first person is especially appropriate when referring to the author's personal observations, experiences, and beliefs, as is the case in Example 6.25.1. The use of "I" in this example is less stilted than using the term *the author* to refer to the writer.

Example 6.25.1

I began to speculate on the origins of this problem during my three years as an assistant to a teacher of the learning disabled.

Frequent use of the first person throughout the introduction and elsewhere in a research report, however, can be distracting. It is especially inappropriate when referring to matters that are not personal, such as the lack of experimental studies mentioned in Example 6.25.2.

Example 6.25.2

When I realized that all the previous research on this topic was nonexperimental, I decided that it would be especially important for me to conduct an experimental study for the current investigation.

Improved Version of Example 6.25.2

Because all the previous research on this topic was nonexperimental, it seemed especially important to conduct an experimental study for the current investigation.

➤ Guideline 6.26 In long literature reviews, start with a paragraph that describes their organization and use subheadings.

The numbered topics in the example near the beginning of this chapter (Example 6.5.1; e.g., Importance of question-asking by children and Introduction to two basic types of questions) could be used as subheadings within the literature review.

In theses and dissertations, where introductions and literature reviews each are usually fairly long chapters, the use of subheadings is especially desirable. Begin each chapter with an overview of what is covered in it, and begin each subsection with such an overview. This is illustrated in Example

6.26.1, in which the first paragraph provides an overview of the chapter, and the second paragraph provides an overview of the first subsection. The third paragraph then begins a discussion of the topic covered by the first subsection with citations to the literature (i.e., "Two major studies...").

Example 6.26.1

CHAPTER 2

LITERATURE REVIEW

This chapter describes literature relevant to the research purposes of this thesis. It is organized into four sections: (1) the importance of question-asking by children, (2) an introduction to two basic types of questions, (3) the relationship between parents' and children's verbal behavior, and (4) the relationship between culture and verbal behavior. At the end of each section, the relevance of the literature to the research reported in this thesis is discussed.

Importance of Question-Asking by Children

Most of the literature on the importance of question-asking deals with the behavior of students in school settings during learning activities. This literature is reviewed first in order to establish the importance of question-asking as a tool in the learning/teaching process. Then, the more limited literature on the importance of question-asking by children as a functional skill in the home and other nonschool settings is reviewed. Throughout, there is an emphasis on the principles of learning theories as well as theories of social interaction that underlie the literature.

Two major studies examined the relationship between students' question-asking behavior and....

> **Guideline 6.27   Consider ending long and complex literature reviews with a brief summary.**

This guideline is illustrated in Example 6.27.1.

Example 6.27.1

In summary, key theoretical models and empirical research findings implicate both negative affect and peer factors in adolescent body attitudes and eating behaviors. Negative affect has been linked to body image and eating problems in some studies, but it has not emerged as a consistent predictor of disordered eating.[15]

Concluding Comments

If you lack confidence in your ability to write introductions and literature reviews, follow these suggestions:

1. Write a topic outline, as illustrated in Example 6.5.1, and take it with you when you consult with your instructor or committee. The outline

---

[15] Hutchinson, Rapee, & Taylor (2010, p. 494).

will help them understand what you are trying to accomplish and make it easier for them to offer guidance.

2. Read numerous reviews of literature, paying attention to how they are organized and how the authors make transitions from one topic to another.

3. After writing a first draft, have it reviewed by friends and colleagues—even if they are not experts on the topic of the review. Ask them to point out elements that are not clear. Note that effective introductions and literature reviews are usually comprehensible to any intelligent layperson.

4. Be prepared to revise and rewrite. Because effective writing is achieved through revising and rewriting, expect your instructor, committee, or journal editor to request revisions.

Exercise for Chapter 6

Because the application of many of the guidelines in this chapter involves a certain amount of subjectivity, there may be some legitimate differences of opinion on the best answers to some of the following questions.

PART A

1. "In theses and dissertations, literature reviews are selective, including references only to the most relevant literature." According to this chapter, is this statement true *or* false?

2. What is wrong with preparing a list of annotations and using it as a literature review (i.e., what does a list of annotations fail to do)?

3. To implement Guideline 6.5, what should be done first?

4. "It is logical to place research hypotheses, objectives, or questions at the beginning of a literature review." According to this chapter, is this statement true *or* false?

5. Critique the following paragraph, which was submitted by a student to indicate the importance of the research topic, which is the prevalence of depression among inner-city adolescents.

"In the new millennium, the public is increasingly aware of the importance of the psychological well-being of all citizens. Because of this recognition by the public, it is important to conduct more studies that shed light on the prevalence of well-being, starting with the psychological well-being of adolescents, who will soon be adults."

6. Showing that many individuals are affected by a problem helps to establish what?

7. According to this chapter, is it important to be able to show that a research project is theory-based?

8. When is pointing out gaps in the literature especially important?

9. How can a student prepare to justify statements regarding gaps in the literature?

10. A student wrote a literature review with a large number of quotations from the literature in the belief that the quotations would substantiate the points being made. According to this chapter, is this appropriate? Explain.

11. According to this chapter, should citations to older literature be avoided?

12. According to this chapter, is it ever appropriate to cite prior literature reviews?

13. Does the following statement cited using the author-date method emphasize "authorship" *or* "content"? Explain.

    "The superiority of the Alpha method for teaching secondary-level science has recently been demonstrated in an experiment with randomized experimental and control groups (Doe, 2011)."

14. Critique the following statement from a literature review.

    "Dr. Richard Doe (2010), professor of education at Stanford University and former head of research for the New York Public Schools, reported on the effects of variable schedules of reinforcement on the mathematics achievement of...."

15. Critique the following statement from a literature review.

"These two experiments unequivocally prove that the XYX method is superior...."

16. Is the use of the first person ever acceptable?

PART B

17. Examine the literature reviews of three research reports published in journals, theses, or dissertations on a topic of interest to you, and answer the following questions.

A. In how many instances does the author explicitly state why the research topic is important and cite specific numbers or percentages to support the statement? If any, copy one statement, and bring it to class for discussion.

B. In how many instances does the author cite references to relevant theories? If any, what are the names of the theories? Are the discussions of the theories brief or in-depth?

C. Overall, do the authors use terminology that reflects the tentative nature of empirical data? (See Guideline 6.23.)

D. In how many cases are direct quotations from the literature included? If any, are there many quotations?

PART C: Write a brief topic outline for a literature review for a research project of interest to you. Have it reviewed by two friends or colleagues, and revise it in light of their comments. Bring it to class for discussion.

Chapter 7
Writing Definitions

Two types of definitions are usually found in empirical research reports. A *conceptual definition*, which resembles dictionary definitions, indicates the general meaning of a concept. These are usually presented in the introduction and/or literature review. *Operational definitions*, which define traits in concrete, step-by-step physical terms, are usually presented in the section on methods. (See Example 1.7.1 in Chapter 1 to review the structure of a basic research report.)

This chapter presents guidelines on what to define and how to write both conceptual and operational definitions.

➤ Guideline 7.1 All variables in a research hypothesis, objective, or question should be defined.

Example 7.1.1 is a hypothesis. "Newspaper reading habits" and "cultural literacy" need to be defined in the research report.

Example 7.1.1

It is hypothesized that there is a direct relationship between newspaper reading habits and cultural literacy.

At the conceptual level, "newspaper reading habits" might be generally defined in terms of "regularity of referring to newspapers for information and entertainment."

At the operational (i.e., physical) level, the definition might refer to the daily average number of minutes spent reading newspapers, the typical number of newspaper sections examined, the number of newspaper stories read, whether individuals subscribe to a newspaper, how often individuals examine newspaper Web sites, and so on.

Obviously, how newspaper reading habits are defined at the operational level could have an important influence on the results of the study for the hypothesis in Example 7.1.1. For instance, using "number of minutes spent reading newspapers" as the operational definition might yield different data than using "how often individuals examine newspaper Web sites."

➢ **Guideline 7.2   The defining attributes of a population (also called *control variables*) should be defined.**

In the hypothesis in Example 7.2.1, "adult education learners" is a defining attribute that should be specifically defined.

Example 7.2.1

There is a direct relationship between newspaper reading habits and cultural literacy among adult education learners.

In Example 7.2.2, the definition of "adult education learners" is not as specific as it might be. The improved version contains more details than the original version. These details help readers understand the characteristics of the population.

Example 7.2.2

"Adult education learners" are adults enrolled in formal education programs.

Improved Version of Example 7.2.2

"Adult education learners" are individuals over 18 years of age who are enrolled in one or more classes in adult schools operated by the Los Angeles Unified School District.

➢ **Guideline 7.3   Key concepts in theories on which the research is based should be defined.**

The "stress-coping theory" is mentioned in Example 7.3.1. (Note that the researchers provide a reference where more information on the theory can be found.)

Example 7.3.1

The stress-coping theory of addictive behaviors (Wills & Shiffman, 1985) has been successfully applied to alcohol abuse and has the potential to increase understanding of gambling.[1]

The researchers who wrote Example 7.3.1 devote seven paragraphs to a description of the tenets of this theory. In addition, they present the definitions of these two psychological constructs that underlie the theory: "stress" and "coping." For instance, they define a particular type of coping in Example 7.3.2. Notice the use of an example in parentheses to help readers understand the definition.

---

[1] Lightsey & Hulsey (2002, p. 202).

Example 7.3.2

Escape-avoidance coping consists of avoiding a stressful situation by engaging in a task not related to the stressor (e.g., drinking alcohol instead of interacting with the family).[2]

➤ Guideline 7.4   A conceptual definition should be sufficiently specific to differentiate it from related concepts.

Even though a conceptual definition indicates only the general meaning of a concept, the conceptual definition should be sufficiently specific to differentiate it from related concepts. Consider Example 7.4.1, which appeared in the literature review of a research article on dual-earner families. In the example, the researchers differentiate between "role overload" and "role interference."

Example 7.4.1

We define role overload as a time-based form of role conflict in which one perceives that the collective demands of multiple roles exceed available time and energy resources, thereby making an individual unable to fulfill adequately the requirements of various roles...unlike role interference, which arises because of mutually incompatible role demands from multiple senders, role overload is related to the totality of time demands placed on an individual....[3]

➤ Guideline 7.5   Consider quoting published conceptual definitions.

As indicated by Guideline 6.17 in the previous chapter, direct quotations from literature should be used sparingly. Quoting definitions, however, is not only acceptable, it can be superior to creating new definitions if the quoted definitions have been carefully thought out and reviewed by other experts, which is often the case in journal articles that have been critiqued by an editorial board.

The author of Example 7.5.1 quotes a definition of "disappearance."

Example 7.5.1

Disappearance is defined as "the arrest, detention, abduction or any other form of deprivation of liberty by agents of the State...followed by a refusal to acknowledge the deprivation of liberty or by concealment of the fate or whereabouts of the disappeared person" (UN Convention on Enforced Disappearance, 2006, Article 2). In practice, it is most often a mechanism for states to kill opponents covertly.[4]

---

[2] Ibid (p. 202).
[3] Higgins, Duxbury, & Lyons (2010, pp. 847–848).
[4] Robins (2010, p. 253).

➢ **Guideline 7.6   Consider providing examples to amplify conceptual definitions.**

Providing one or more examples can often make the meaning of a definition clear. In Example 7.3.2, the researchers provide a parenthetical example. In Example 7.5.1, the researcher amplifies the conceptual definition by providing an example in the last sentence.

➢ **Guideline 7.7   Operational definitions usually should be provided in the Method section of a report.**

An operational definition is one that is stated in terms of physical steps. While conceptual definitions are often presented in the introduction/literature review, operational definitions are usually presented in the section on methods.[5] (See Example 1.7.1 in Chapter 1 to review the structure of a basic research report.)

It is especially important to provide operational definitions within the *Measures* subsection of the section on methods in order to operationalize measurement procedures. Compare Example 7.7.1 with its improved version. The improved version has been operationalized by referring to the physical steps used to measure the variable of "desire for thinness."

Example 7.7.1

Desire for thinness was determined based on the girls' ratings of themselves in relation to silhouette drawings of very thin to very fat girls.

Improved Version of Example 7.7.1

Desire for thinness was measured with the girls' version of the Children's Figure Rating Scale (Tiggemann & Wilson-Barrett, 1998). This scale presents on an A3-sized bright-colored piece of cardboard with nine young female silhouette drawings, ranging from very thin to very fat. Girls were asked, "Which girl do you think you look like?" (current figure), followed by "Which girl would you most like to look like?" (ideal figure). Girls responded by simply pointing to their choices. Desire for thinness was calculated as current minus ideal figure rating. Good test–retest reliability has been found for such figure rating scales with children as young as 6 to 7 years of age (Collins, 1991).[6]

In reports on experiments, the steps taken to treat the experimental groups should be operationalized in the section on methods. Compare Example 7.7.2, which is not very operational, with its improved version, which describes physical conditions and steps.

---

[5] Another arrangement is to provide both conceptual and operational definitions in the section on methods.
[6] Dohnt & Tiggemann (2006, p. 930).

Example 7.7.2

The stress-producing condition for the experimental group was a mild verbal threat given by the experimenter.

Improved Version of Example 7.7.2

In order to produce the stress-producing condition for the experimental group, a male experimenter dressed in a white doctor's jacket seated the participants. He introduced himself as a physician with a specialty in internal medicine and stated that for the purposes of the experiment, "You will receive a mild electric shock while we measure your blood pressure."

➢ Guideline 7.8 Consider providing operational definitions for each conceptual definition.

For each conceptual definition, consider providing an operational definition in the section on methods. A conceptual definition of a "hate crime" and a corresponding operational definition are provided in Example 7.8.1.

Example 7.8.1

Conceptual definition in the Introduction:

Bias is a preformed negative attitude toward a group based on race, religion, ethnicity/national origin, sexual orientation, or disability status. A *bias crime*, also known as a *hate crime*, is a criminal offense committed against person or property that is motivated, in whole or in part, by the offender's bias.

Corresponding operational definition in the Method section:

It is acknowledged that some hate crimes reported to law enforcement were not reported to [the FBI] and that other hate crimes were not reported to any local law enforcement agency. However, data used in this analysis represented the complete universe of hate crimes *that have been properly reported to the FBI* as required by the Hate Crimes Statistics Act.[7]

Notice that the conceptual definition in Example 7.8.1 allows for hate crimes to be operationally defined in many ways, such as surveying individuals to see if they believe they have been the victims of hate crimes or relying on local or state statistics. In Example 7.8.1, the operational definition is sufficiently specific that it rules out alternative methods of defining the variable. Also, note that reporting crimes to the FBI and obtaining the data from the FBI are physical acts that operationalize the variable.

---

[7] McMahon, West, Lewis, Armstrong, & Conway (2004, pp. 68–69).

➢ Guideline 7.9 If a published measure was used, the variable measured by it may be operationally defined by citing reference(s).

A published measure,[8] such as an achievement test, almost always comes with specific, step-by-step physical directions for its use. By citing the test with a reference to the author and publisher of the test, a researcher can provide an operational definition. Example 7.9.1 provides such a definition.

Example 7.9.1

Beginning mathematics skill was defined as the composite score on Form S of the Primary Level 2 multiple-choice/open-ended Mathematics Test of the Stanford Achievement Test Series, Tenth Edition (Harcourt Brace, 2008).

To further operationalize the definition in Example 7.9.1, the author could provide an overview of the physical properties of the test (e.g., content of the items, numbers of multiple-choice and open-ended items, time limits, and the statistical properties of the test, especially reliability and validity.

➢ Guideline 7.10 If an unpublished measure was used, consider reproducing sample questions or the entire measure.

For specialized research purposes, researchers often construct their own measures (e.g., tests, scales, and checklists). If such a measure is very short, a copy may be included in the research report. Longer measures should be included in appendices in term projects, theses, and dissertations, but usually are not included in research reports published in journal articles. Authors of journal articles should be prepared to supply copies of longer, unpublished measures to readers who request them.

Examples 7.10.1 and 7.10.2 illustrate this guideline.

Example 7.10.1

Eating Behaviors. The Eating Attitude Test…is an objective self-report measure where respondents were asked to rate the frequency of each behavior (e.g., "avoid foods with sugars in them," "vomit after I have eaten," "feel extremely guilty after eating," "engage in dieting behavior") on a 6-point scale, ranging from "never" to "always."[9]

Example 7.10.2

Family Life Issues. Open-ended questions pertaining to a wide range of family life issues…were asked. Examples of specific questions or statements included "Tell me about how this neighborhood/area is as a place to live."; "Why or why isn't your housing adequate for you and your family's needs?"; "Tell me about your

---

[8] In research, the term *instruments* is synonymous with the term *measures*.
[9] Sira & Ballard (2009, pp. 215–216).

work history."; and "If you needed help with transportation or car repairs, how often could you count on getting help from family, friends, or others who don't live with you?"[10]

➢ Guideline 7.11 Operational definitions should be specific enough so that another researcher can replicate the study.

A *replication* is an attempt to reproduce the results of a previous study by using the same research methods. Replicability is the major criterion for judging the reliability and validity of the results of empirical research.

Even definitions that appear to be highly operational at first glance may be inadequate when a researcher attempts to replicate a study. The definition in Example 7.11.1 illustrates this point. When a researcher prepares to replicate a study involving "visual acuity," questions about the physical process arise: How large were the letters? What type of screen was used? What type of film was used to produce the letters? and so on. Answers to these questions could easily affect individuals' ability to recognize letters of the alphabet flashed on a screen.

Example 7.11.1

Visual acuity was defined as the ability to name the letters of the alphabet when flashed on a screen in a random order for a period of two seconds for each letter.

This guideline is often not followed to the letter. In practice, a writer should consider how operational a definition needs to be to permit a reasonably close replication. For making fine discriminations among very similar shapes, answers to the questions posed about Example 7.11.1 may be crucial to a successful replication.

➢ Guideline 7.12 Even a highly operational definition may not be a useful definition.

An operational definition that is too narrow or is too different from how most other individuals define a variable may be inadequate. Example 7.12.1 illustrates this point. It provides a fairly operational definition of self-concept, but the definition is much narrower than that used by most psychologists and teachers.

Example 7.12.1

Self-concept was defined as the number of times each child smiled during the first 15 minutes of homeroom for five consecutive days. A smile was defined as a noticeable upward turn where the lips meet—based on agreement by three independent observers. Each observer was a graduate student in clinical psychology.

---

[10] Greder et al. (2009, p. 191).

Counts of smiles were made from video recordings, which permitted the observers to reexamine facial expressions that were questionable.

Concluding Comments

Writing satisfactory operational definitions is sometimes more difficult than it might at first appear. When writing them, assume that you are telling someone exactly how to conduct your study. Then have the first draft of the definitions reviewed by colleagues and ask them if they could perform the same study in the same way without requesting additional information.

As a general rule, it is best to provide lengthy, detailed operational definitions so that readers can be confident that they understand them.

Exercise for Chapter 7

PART A: For each of the following definitions, describe what additional types of information, if any, are needed to make it more operational.

1. Language skill was defined as scores on a scale from 1 to 10 on an essay test that required students to write three essays in a 50-minute class period.

2. Depression was defined as the raw score on the Second Edition of Doe's Depression Inventory for Adults (Doe, 2010).

3. Computer phobia was defined as clear signs of anxiety when being seated in front of a computer.

4. Hispanic students were defined as those students whose surnames appeared on a master list of Hispanic/Latino(a) surnames developed by the author in consultation with a linguist. This list may be obtained by writing to the author at P.O. Box xxx, Any City, State, Zip Code.

5. Potential high school dropouts were defined as those who have a poor attitude toward school.

6. Discrimination was defined as acts against individuals that limit their opportunities solely because of preconceived biases against the groups to which the individuals belong.

PART B: For each of the following variables, write a highly operational definition. Because you may not have studied some of these variables, do not concern yourself with whether your definitions are highly useful. (See Guideline 7.12.) Instead, make them sufficiently operational so that they would make a study of them replicable. (See Guideline 7.11.)

7. Political involvement

8. Math anxiety

9. Ability to form friendships

10. Desire to achieve in school

PART C: Name a variable you might want to study. Write a conceptual definition and a highly operational definition of it. (For this activity, do not cite a published test or scale in order to define the variable you have selected.) Have the first draft of your definitions reviewed by colleagues, and then revise them. Bring both drafts of the two definitions to class for discussion.

PART D: Examine three research articles in journals, theses, or dissertations. Note how the variables are defined. Copy the definition you think is most operational, and bring it to class for discussion.

Notes

Chapter 8
Writing Assumptions, Limitations, and Delimitations

An *assumption* is a condition that is believed to be true even though the direct evidence of its truth is either absent or very limited. A *limitation* is a weakness or handicap that potentially limits the validity of the results, while a *delimitation* is a boundary to which a study was deliberately confined.

Authors of research reports published in journal articles often integrate statements of assumptions, limitations, and delimitations in various sections of their articles, including the Introduction, Method section, and very frequently in the Discussion section at the end of the report. These authors usually are very selective in deciding which ones to state, naming only the major ones. Students who are writing term projects, theses, and dissertations are often expected to discuss these issues in some detail in order to show that they understand the concepts. In theses and dissertations, the assumptions, limitations, and delimitations are sometimes described in separate subsections of one of the chapters—often, the first chapter or the last chapter.

➤ Guideline 8.1   When stating an assumption, consider providing the reason(s) why it was necessary to make the assumption.

In Example 8.1.1, this guideline has not been followed because, while it states what was assumed, it does not state why the assumption was necessary. Because no measure of human behavior is perfectly valid, Example 8.1.1 adds little to the research report. In the first sentence of the improved version, the authors describe the circumstances that led to the use of a scale that may have limited validity.

Example 8.1.1
It was assumed that the cheerfulness scale was valid.

Improved Version of Example 8.1.1
Because we did not have the resources to make direct observations and ratings of cheerfulness over time in a variety of settings, we constructed a self-report measure of cheerfulness. It was necessary to assume that the participants were honest in self-reporting their typical levels of cheerfulness. To encourage honest responses, the cheerfulness scale was administered anonymously, and the partici-

pants were encouraged to be open and honest by the research assistant who administered the survey.

> ## Guideline 8.2 If there is a reason for believing that an assumption is true, state the reason.

The last sentence in the improved version of Example 8.1.1 suggests a basis for believing that the assumption is true. Likewise, the last sentence in Example 8.2.1 provides the basis for such a belief.

Example 8.2.1

Because the investigator could not be present in all the classrooms while the experimental method was being used, it was necessary to assume that the teachers consistently and conscientiously used the experimental method of instruction. This assumption seems tenable because the teachers were given intensive training in the method, as described in the Method section of this report, and they reported enthusiasm for the method, as described in the Results section.

> ## Guideline 8.3 If an assumption is highly questionable, consider casting it as a limitation.

Example 8.3.1 refers to a common flaw in research: use of a small sample. Unless a researcher has some empirical basis for believing that those in the small sample are representative of the larger population, it would be better to describe this problem as a limitation, as is done in the improved version. Note that researchers should not use assumptions to "wish away" fundamental flaws.

Example 8.3.1

It is assumed that the results we obtained with our small sample are generalizable to the larger population.

Improved Version of Example 8.3.1

There are several limitations in this study. The sample was small and involved youth in only one detention center....[1]

> ## Guideline 8.4 Distinguish between limitations and delimitations.

As indicated at the beginning of this chapter, a *limitation* is a weakness or handicap that potentially limits the validity of the results, while a *delimitation* is a boundary to which a study was deliberately confined.

To understand the difference between a limitation and a delimitation, consider a researcher who wants to study artistic creativity in general but

---

[1] Lopez-Williams, Stoep, Kuo, & Stewart (2006, p. 277).

uses only a measure of creative drawing. This would be a limitation because it is a weakness in the execution of the study (i.e., measuring only creative drawing when the purpose is to study artistic creativity in general). In contrast, if the researcher's purpose is only to study creative drawing and the researcher deliberately chooses a measure of creative drawing, the findings would be delimited to this type of creativity, which is not a flaw in light of the researcher's purpose.

➢ Guideline 8.5   Discuss limitations and delimitations separately.

Because they are separate issues, discuss the limitations (methodological weaknesses or flaws) in separate paragraphs or sections from delimitations (boundaries to which the study was deliberately limited).

➢ Guideline 8.6   Consider elaborating on the nature of a limitation.

Instead of merely stating that the small sample was a limitation of their study, the authors of Example 8.6.1 elaborate in their discussion of this limitation.

Example 8.6.1

Due to the small numbers of respondents working in practice settings such as long-term-care facilities, public health units, and mental health clinics, responses were grouped and reported under one category ("other") to ensure the confidentiality of respondents. This impeded us from exploring and revealing similarities and differences in NP practices among these settings and with the other practice settings.[2]

➢ Guideline 8.7   Consider speculating on the possible effects of a limitation on the results of a study.

The authors of Example 8.7.1 speculate that their results may underestimate drug use because the data were collected via face-to-face interviews. The tendency of people to underreport illegal activities is a limitation of the interview method, which can be overcome, in part, by using confidential, anonymous questionnaires.[3]

---

[2] Koren, Mian, & Rukholm (2010, p. 66).
[3] Of course, interviews have some advantages over questionnaires, such as providing more flexibility and allowing researchers to probe for additional information.

Example 8.7.1

Our findings have several limitations.... As with other interviewer-administered surveys, it is possible that personal behaviors and illegal activities such as drug use may have been underreported. Hence, our survey would have underestimated the prevalence of drug use.[4]

➢ Guideline 8.8   If a study has serious limitations, consider labeling it a pilot study.

A *pilot study* is an exploratory study that is used to try out and refine instruments, see if participants will be cooperative, check for preliminary support for a hypothesis, and so on. When this guideline is followed, it is sometimes done in the title, with a subtitle such as "A Pilot Study."

Researchers who conduct pilot studies often mention this status in several places in their research reports. For instance, the researchers who conducted the study cited in Example 8.8.1 mentioned that they conducted a pilot study in the title, in the Abstract, and in the Discussion section of their report.

Example 8.8.1

"Pilot study" mentioned in the title: A Pilot Study Examining Exercise Self-Efficacy as a Mediator for Walking Behavior in College-Age Women

"Pilot study" mentioned in the Abstract: This pilot study examined the possible mediation of walking behavior by exercise self-efficacy in an Internet-delivered intervention in a sample of college-age women.

"Pilot study" mentioned in the Discussion section: In this pilot study, the hypothesis was that changes in exercise self-efficacy would mediate changes in walking behavior.[5]

➢ Guideline 8.9   Consider pointing out strengths as well as limitations.

While it is important to warn readers of the limitations of a study, it is equally important to point out special strengths that make the study noteworthy. While this may be done in various sections of a report, it is often appropriate to point out strengths immediately before or after describing limitations, which are most often described in the Discussion section. (See Example 1.7.1 in Chapter 1 to review the structure of basic research reports.)

In Example 8.9.1, the author describes how her study improves on previous research, which is a strength of her study.

---

[4] Thiede et al. (2003, p. 1920).
[5] Ornes & Ransdell (2010, pp. 1098–1102).

Example 8.9.1

Inconsistent results of previous studies suggest that our understanding of these associations is far from complete. Specifically, prior research has three major limitations that the present study improves on. First, this study takes into account lineage by analyzing young adults' relationships with all available grandparents, which has not been done before....[6]

Exercise for Chapter 8

PART A

1. Suppose a researcher mailed a questionnaire to each member of a population but only 18% completed and returned the questionnaires. Further, suppose the researcher has no information on how the nonrespondents differ from the respondents. In your opinion, should the researcher assume that the sample is sound *or* should the researcher state that the nonresponse rate is a limitation? Explain.

2. Suppose a researcher's purpose was to examine adolescent girls' knowledge of nutrition. If the researcher included only adolescent girls as participants in the study (i.e., excluding adolescent boys), should the inclusion of only adolescent girls be considered a "limitation" *or* a "delimitation"?

3. Suppose a researcher used a standardized test that had been validated for the type of population being studied. Furthermore, suppose the test had high validity but, as with all tests, was somewhat less than perfectly valid. In your opinion, should the researcher describe this circumstance as a limitation? Would it be reasonable for the researcher to assume that the test is valid? Why?

PART B

4. Consider a research project that you plan to undertake. If you know of an assumption you would probably need to make, write a statement describing it.

---

[6] Monserud (2010, pp. 40–41).

5. Consider a research project you plan to undertake. If you know of a limitation (i.e., methodological flaw) that you would probably have if you conducted the study, write a statement describing it. For the same study, describe a delimitation to which your study probably would be confined.

PART C

6. Examine two research reports published in journals, theses, or dissertations that contain explicit statements of assumptions and/or limitations. Copy their relevant portions and bring them to class for discussion.

7. How many of the individual assumptions/limitations that you examined for Question 6 involved sampling? How many involved the instruments? How many involved other issues? Name them.

Chapter 9
Writing Method Sections

The Method section follows the literature review. (See Example 1.7.1 in Chapter 1 to review the structure of a basic research report.) The section on methods describes the steps taken to gather data.

➤ Guideline 9.1   First, describe the participants.

Immediately under the main heading of "Method" (centered in bold) should appear the subheading "Participants" (flush left in bold). As indicated in the next guideline, the term *Subjects* may be substituted for *Participants* under certain circumstances.

A portion of Example 1.4.1 in Chapter 1 is reproduced here as Example 9.1.1 to show the placement of the material on participants (see the arrow in the example).

Example 9.1.1

Title in Upper- and Lowercase Letters
Abstract (a main heading; centered in bold)
A literature review that introduces the research problem (with no heading)
Method (a main heading; centered in bold)
⇨**Participants** (a subheading; flush left in bold)
Measures (a subheading; flush left in bold)

➤ Guideline 9.2   Decide whether to use the term *participants* or *subjects* to refer to the individuals studied.

Subjects is the traditional term used to refer to individuals studied in empirical research. Increasingly, researchers are using the term *participants* to refer to these individuals.[1]

When individuals freely consent to participate in a study, it is logical to call them participants instead of subjects. However, sometimes researchers conduct research without obtaining consent. A clear example is a study of animal behavior, in which case it makes sense to refer to the animals as *subjects* in a report of the research.

---

[1] Other terms that are sometimes used are *respondents* (e.g., to refer to individuals who respond to a mailed questionnaire) and *examinees* (e.g., to refer to individuals who are participating in test development research). Qualitative researchers sometimes prefer the term *informants*.

Some studies of humans also do not involve consent to participate. For instance, if a researcher is conducting an observational study of the behavior of adolescents in a large shopping mall, the researcher might not need consent to observe these public behaviors. In a report of such a study, the term *subjects* is more appropriate than the term *participants* because the adolescents are not knowingly participating and, of course, have not consented to participate.

➢ **Guideline 9.3   Describe the informed consent procedures, if any.**

Institutions such as colleges and universities, as well as funding sources such as government agencies, usually require researchers to obtain informed consent from the individuals who will be participating in research studies. This is done with a consent form. A basic consent form describes the purpose of the study, the possible benefits and harm that might result from participation, and the identification of those who are conducting the research. Potential participants are asked to sign the form acknowledging that they freely agree to participate and that they understand that they are free to withdraw from the study at any time without penalty.[2]

Example 9.3.1 illustrates how to briefly describe the use of informed consent in a research report. Note that the authors indicate that all those contacted signed the form. If the rate is less than 100%, the percentage or the number that signed (and, therefore, participated in the research) should be reported.

Example 9.3.1

Participants were 108 undergraduates enrolled in an introductory sociology course. Each was given an informed consent form, which had been approved by the university's institutional research review board. The form indicated that (1) the study concerned attitudes toward road rage, (2) the students were not required to participate, and (3) if they did participate, they could withdraw from the study at any time without penalty. All students signed the form and participated fully.

When minors are participants, informed consent should be obtained from parents or guardians. This process should be described in the research report. Example 9.3.2 indicates how this might be done.

Example 9.3.2

Parental consent was obtained by sending the student home with a consent form to be signed by the parent and returned to school by the student. Students were given another form to take home if the original was lost or misplaced. The class that returned the highest number of consent forms was given a party as a group incentive.

---

[2] Precise requirements for preparing an informed consent form should be obtained from the appropriate institution or funding agency.

It was not possible to send out repeated waves of the consent forms or to make contact with parents due to the large number of schools and the proximity of data collection to the end of the school year (Swaim et al., 2001).[3]

> ## Guideline 9.4 Consider describing steps taken to maintain confidentiality of the data.

Participants have the right to expect that the data they provide will remain confidential. Some researchers describe the steps they have taken in order to maintain confidentiality of the data, as illustrated in Example 9.4.1.

Example 9.4.1

In order to maintain confidentiality, the questionnaires were administered in the school cafeteria by a research assistant rather than by the teachers. Although the teachers were present, they were instructed not to walk around the cafeteria to observe students' responses because of the sensitive nature of some of the questions. In addition, after completing the questionnaires, students folded them in half and put them into a ballot box as they filed out of the cafeteria. At no time were the teachers allowed to examine the questionnaires. As soon as the data were recorded on data collection forms and double-checked, the questionnaires were shredded. They were destroyed because some of the extended responses on the questionnaires contained information that could be used to identify individual respondents.

> ## Guideline 9.5 The participants should be described in enough detail for the reader to visualize them.

Example 9.5.1 helps readers visualize the participants' neighborhood, gender, age, grade level, and racial/ethnic self-identifications. Note that the detailed description of racial/ethnic characteristics is especially appropriate because the study from which the example was drawn dealt with urban adolescents' perceived support for challenging racism, sexism, and social injustice from peers, family, and community members.

Example 9.5.1

Ninety-eight students at two urban high schools in the northeastern United States served as the sample for this study. These participants attended inner-city high schools that are composed predominantly of students of color from poor and working class urban neighborhoods; the final sample consisted of 56 females and 42 males. The mean age for all participants was 15.44 (SD = .96); 48 of the participants were in the ninth grade (49%) and 50 in the tenth grade (51%). The ethnic and racial self-identifications were as follows: 18.4% (18) self-identified as Black/African American/African/Cape Verdean; 20.4% (20) as Black/Caribbean; 35.7% (35) as Latino/a; 5.1% (5) as White, European, or European American; 4.1% (4) as Asian; 2% (2) as Middle Eastern/Arabic; and 14.3% (14) as multi-

---

[3] McNamara, Swaim, & Rosén (2010, pp. 112–113).

ethnic/racial. The racial/ethnic demographics of our participants correspond to the racial/ethnic demographics of these two schools.[4]

Because the number of characteristics that might be used to describe participants is almost limitless, researchers should be selective in deciding on which ones to report. As a general rule, describe those that are most relevant to the issues being studied. For instance, in a study on physicians' attitudes toward assisted suicide, "religious background" would be a relevant characteristic. For a study on algebra achievement, it would not be relevant.

➤ Guideline 9.6 Consider reporting demographics in tables.

Tables such as the one in Example 9.6.1 make it easy for readers to scan the information that describes the participants. Note the use of the term *demographic characteristics* in the title of the table. These are background characteristics that help readers visualize the participants.

Example 9.6.1

Table 1
Demographic Characteristics of the Participants

Characteristic	Number	Percent
Gender		
Girl	81	72
Boy	31	28
Current grade level		
Third	16	14
Fourth	37	33
Fifth	55	49
Sixth	4	4
Qualify for subsidized school lunch program?		
Yes	99	88
No	13	12
Family status		
Living with both parents	72	64
Living with one parent	35	31
Living with neither parent	5	4

➤ Guideline 9.7 When a sample is very small, consider providing a description of individual participants.

The information on a small number of individuals can be presented in a paragraph or in a table, as in Example 9.7.1.

---

[4] Diemer, Kauffman, Koenig, Trahan, & Hsieh (2006, p. 449).

Example 9.7.1

Table 1
Select Demographic Characteristics and Psychiatric Diagnoses
of the Participants

Client	Age	Sex	Psychiatric diagnosis
1	19	M	Conduct disorder
			Attention deficit disorder
			Learning disability
2	20	M	Dysthymic disorder
3	20	M	Major depression
4	20	F	Major depression
5	21	M	Conduct disorder
6	22	F	Dysthymic disorder

➢ **Guideline 9.8 If only a sample was studied, the method of sampling should be described.**

Sometimes, researchers study entire populations (e.g., the entire sets of individuals in which the researchers are interested). More often, they sample from a population, study the sample, and then generalize (i.e., infer that what is true of the sample is also true of the population).

When sampling is conducted, the researchers should name the population from which the sample was drawn and indicate the method used to draw the sample (e.g., simple random sampling). Example 9.8.1 illustrates how this might be done.

Example 9.8.1

From the population of all registered nurses in public hospitals in Texas, 120 were selected using simple random sampling.

When a researcher draws a sample of convenience (very often students at the college or university where the researcher is employed), this fact should be explicitly mentioned, as in Example 9.8.2.

Example 9.8.2

A convenience sample consisting of 42 women and 34 men participated in this study. All participants were enrolled as students at a large public university in the southwestern United States. The participants were volunteers who had responded to a flyer seeking participants to take part in a study of sibling rivalry. The flyer indicated that the study would take about 45 minutes and that an honorarium of $10 would be paid to each participant.

➤ **Guideline 9.9 Explicitly acknowledge weaknesses in sampling.**

When the method of sampling is clearly deficient, such as the one in Example 9.8.2, it is a good idea for the author to acknowledge this fact with a sentence such as "Because a sample of convenience was used, generalizations to populations should be made with extreme caution," or "The use of volunteers as participants in this study greatly restricts the generalizability of the results." Inclusion of statements such as these is especially important in student projects, theses, and dissertations. In their absence, instructors may not know whether students are aware of this important limitation.[5]

➤ **Guideline 9.10 Provide detailed information on nonparticipants when possible.**

Information on individuals who refuse to participate in a study is often available and usually should be reported. For instance, in a study on achievement in a school setting, the cumulative records of nonparticipating students might be accessed so that average standardized test scores for those who participated and those who declined to participate can be reported.

The researcher who wrote Example 9.10.1 sent letters soliciting participation to all families referred to a program for child abuse prevention, but only 26% of them participated in the study. The information in the last sentence of the example helps reassure readers that nonparticipants are not substantially different from participants (i.e., helps reassure them that the participants are not an idiosyncratic subgroup of the population).

Example 9.10.1

Initial recruitment letters were sent, on a rolling basis, to all participants who had been referred to the program within a 12-month period. The letters were sent within 2 months of the referral. A second recruitment letter and a follow-up phone call followed, if needed. In 12 months, 76 referred clients were solicited for research participation; 23 responded that they were interested, with 20 ultimately participating. An analysis of this subgroup yielded no significant differences from the 56 participants who chose not to participate in terms of race, age, number of children, zip code, or socioeconomic status.[6]

➤ **Guideline 9.11 Describe the measures after describing the participants.**

Measures are instruments (such as achievement tests, attitude scales, questionnaires, checklists, and interview schedules).

---

[5] While statements regarding generalizing from a sample are often made in the Method section, many researchers also make them in the Discussion section at the end of the research report. See Chapter 12.
[6] Altman (2003, p. 472).

Immediately under the subheading of "Method" (centered in bold) should appear the subheading "Participants" (flush left in bold). The next subheading is "Measures" (flush left in bold). A portion of Example 1.4.1 in Chapter 1 is reproduced here as Example 9.11.1 to show the placement of the material on measures (see the arrow in the example).

Example 9.11.1

Title in Upper- and Lowercase Letters
Abstract (a main heading; centered in bold)
A literature review that introduces the research problem (with no heading)
Method (a main heading; centered in bold)
Participants (a subheading; flush left in bold)
⇨**Measures** (a subheading; flush left in bold)

> ➢ **Guideline 9.12 Describe the traits a measure was designed to measure, its format, and the possible range of score values.**

Consider Example 9.12.1, which has insufficient detail, and its improved version.

Example 9.12.1

Attitude toward school was measured with a nine-item questionnaire developed for use in this study.

Improved Version of Example 9.12.1

Attitude toward school was measured with a questionnaire developed for use in this study. It contains nine statements. The first three measure attitudes toward academic subjects. The next three measure attitudes toward teachers, counselors, and administrators. The last three measure attitudes toward the social environment in the school. Participants were asked to rate each statement on a five-point scale from 1 (strongly disagree) to 5 (strongly agree). Scores for individual participants could range from 9 (strongly disagreeing with all nine statements) to 45 (strongly agreeing with all statements). The complete questionnaire is shown in Appendix A of this journal article.

Notice these desirable characteristics of the improved version of Example 9.12.1: It indicates (1) the number of items, (2) what the items were designed to measure, (3) the scale (i.e., strongly disagree to strongly agree) that was used, (4) the possible range of scores, and (5) the availability of the complete measure. For long instruments, some researchers do not include the entire measure in the research report, but rather make copies available on request.

➢ **Guideline 9.13 Summarize information on reliability and validity, when available.**

The two most important characteristics of a measure are its *reliability* (consistency of results) and *validity* (the extent to which the measure actually measures what it is designed to measure).

For research projects and journal articles, researchers typically provide only brief summaries of what is known about a measure's reliability and validity, as illustrated in Example 9.13.1, in which the writers refer to the test's internal consistency reliability (known as *alpha* [α = .87]) and predictive validity.

Example 9.13.1

Early cognitive ability was measured using the word analysis achievement tests of the Iowa Test of Basic Skills at the end of kindergarten (α = .87). This measure has been previously correlated to both third- and sixth-grade reading and math achievement, which suggests its predictive validity as a measure of individual developed abilities (Reynolds, 1989, 1991; Reynolds & Bezruczko, 1993).[7]

In Example 9.13.2, the writers summarize information on internal consistency reliability, test-retest reliability (i.e., stability), as well as validity.

Example 9.13.2

Epworth Sleepiness Scale. Both internal consistency reliability (.73–.88) and stability (r = .82) of the ESS have been established (Johns, 1992), with a reliability of .71 obtained in this study. The ESS has been identified as a valid measure of sleep propensity in adults, with the ability to differentiate between groups known to have varying levels of sleepiness, such as healthy adults and patients with narcolepsy or sleep apnea (Johns, 1994).[8]

Students who are writing theses and dissertations may be expected to describe the reliability and validity of the measures they use in considerable detail. They may be expected, for instance, to summarize how the reliability and validity studies were conducted and to interpret the results of these studies in light of any methodological flaws in the studies.

➢ **Guideline 9.14 Provide references where more information on the measures can be found.**

When there is published information on measures, especially on their reliability and validity, provide references to it. This is illustrated in the last sentences in Examples 9.13.1 and 9.13.2 and in Example 9.15.1.

---

[7] Mann & Reynolds (2006, p. 158).
[8] Scott, Hofmeister, Rogness, & Rogers (2010, p. 253–254).

➢ **Guideline 9.15 Consider providing sample items or questions.**

It can be helpful to readers to see sample items (such as test items) or questions (such as interview questions). Example 9.15.1 illustrates how this might be done.

Example 9.15.1

The Positive Bonding Scale was adapted from the Couple Activities Scale (Markman, 2000). It consists of nine questions assessing the friendship, intimacy, fun, felt support, and sensual/sexual relationship of the couple. Example questions include "We regularly have conversations where we just talk as good friends," "We have a satisfying sensual or sexual relationship," "I feel emotionally supported by my partner," and "We regularly make time for fun activities together as a couple." Stanley, Whitton, Kline, and Markman (2006) report logical convergence of the parent scale with other indices of individual and marital functioning.[9]

➢ **Guideline 9.16 Make unpublished measures available.**

Researchers often construct new measures (or modify existing measures) for use in their research. For short measures, consider providing the complete set of items (or questions) in the description of the measure, as is done in Example 9.16.1.

Example 9.16.1

These questions were: (1) Regarding techniques for teaching my child new skills, I feel the individual therapy he/she participated in helped him/her learn... (A) no new skills, (B) a few new skills, (C) some new skills, (D) a reasonable amount of new skills, or (E) many new skills; and (2) Overall, I feel the individual therapy my child participated in was... (A) not at all helpful, (B) a little helpful, (C) somewhat helpful, (D) helpful, or (E) very helpful. Responses to these questions scored between 1 (*not helpful/learned no new skills*) and 5 (*very helpful/learned many new skills*) and summed across both questions for a score ranging between 2 and 10).[10]

For longer measures, consider putting them in a table (instead of providing them in a paragraph) within the subsection on measures. Example 9.16.2 shows a table that was included in a research report. It shows the complete set of questions used in a focus group study.

---

[9] Allen, Rhoades, Stanley, & Markman (2010, p. 283).
[10] Bushman & Peacock (2010, pp. 108–109).

Example 9.16.2

Table 1
Mother Focus-Group Questions[11]

What do you think are the most important things a parent should say about sex to their son or daughter who is in the sixth or seventh grade? What are the topics parents should be talking about?
An issue parents wrestle with is whether to talk with their teens about birth control, like condoms. Some parents fear they are just encouraging their children to have sex if they do so. Others feel that it is important to do so. What do you think? Should parents talk to their sixth- or seventh-grade adolescent child about birth control?
The last thing that some teens want to do is talk with their parents about sex. Why is this? Why do some teens not want to talk about this with their parents?
What are the major reasons you would give your adolescent sixth- or seventh-grade child as to why he or she should not have sexual intercourse at this time in his or her life?
What things should a parent say about sex to a boy that a parent should not say to a girl?
What things should a parent say about sex to a girl that a parent should not say to a boy?
Suppose a mother found out that her son or daughter was having sex. What should she do?
Each of us comes from different cultural backgrounds—from different countries, different ethnic groups, and different religions, and often speaking different languages. How does your cultural background influence how you should talk with your teen about sex?

For longer measures, an alternative to using a table is to put copies of complete measures in an appendix at the end of the research report. When this is done, mention the appendix in the body of the report, which is illustrated in the last sentence of the improved version of Example 9.12.1.

Concluding Comments

This chapter deals with the two questions almost universally addressed under the main heading of Method: (1) Who were the participants? and (2) What measures were used?

The next chapter deals with special issues in describing the methods used in experiments (i.e., studies in which participants are given treatments in order to observe their response to the treatments).

---

[11] Guilamo-Ramos et al. (2006, p. 172).

Exercise for Chapter 9

PART A

1. According to this chapter, when is it logical to refer to individuals studied as *participants*?

2. Should a consent form describe both possible benefits *and* possible harm?

3. Suppose a teacher is writing a research report on the effectiveness of new materials for teaching second-grade math. Name two characteristics of the participants that might be relevant for inclusion in a report on this topic.

4. What are *demographic characteristics*?

5. If a researcher uses a *convenience sample*, should this fact be mentioned in the research report?

6. Is it desirable to provide information on nonparticipants (i.e., those who refuse to participate in a study)?

7. Within the Method section, should "participants" *or* "measures" be described first?

8. Are researchers who write journal articles expected to describe the reliability and validity of the measures they use in considerable detail?

9. What are the two ways for making long, complete measures available?

PART B

10. Locate a description of participants in a research report in a journal article, thesis, or dissertation that you think lacks sufficient detail. Copy it, and briefly describe other types of information that might have been included to give a better picture of the participants. Bring your work to class for discussion.

11. Locate a description of the measures in a research report in a journal article, thesis, or dissertation that describes its reliability and validity. Bring it to class for discussion. (Note that some authors use the subheading "Instrumentation" for the section on measures.)

Chapter 10
Describing Experimental Methods

An *experiment* is a study in which treatments are given in order to determine their effects on participants. A set of treatments (e.g., two levels of dosage of a drug) is known as the *independent variable*, while the outcome (e.g., feeling less pain) is the *dependent variable*.

➢ **Guideline 10.1 Describe experimental methods under the subheading "Procedure" under the main heading of "Method."**

A portion of Example 1.4.1 in Chapter 1 is reproduced here as Example 10.1.1 to show the placement of the material described in this chapter (see the arrow in the example). Note that the previous chapter describes what to include under "Participants" and "Measures," which are also subheadings under "Method."

Example 10.1.1

Title in Upper- and Lowercase Letters
Abstract (a main heading; centered in bold)[1]
A literature review that introduces the research problem (with no heading)
Method (a main heading; centered in bold)
Participants (a subheading; flush left in bold)
Measures (a subheading; flush left in bold)
⇨**Procedure** (optional; a subheading; flush left in bold)

➢ **Guideline 10.2 If there are two or more groups, explicitly state how the groups were formed.**

When two or more groups are to be compared (e.g., comparing an experimental and a control group), random assignment is highly desirable for assignment to groups because it assures that there was no bias in the assignment. Example 10.2.1 illustrates how the use of random assignment might be described.

Example 10.2.1

Before school began in August, each participating student was assigned a number, from 001–151. Using randomization software, the kindergarten students were randomly assigned either to interactive writing ($n = 75$) or to writing workshop ($n = 76$).[2]

---

[1] This heading should usually be used in unpublished papers. In research journals, it is often omitted, with the abstract being identified by its placement at the beginning and by being indented on the left and right.
[2] Jones, Reutzel, & Fargo (2010, p. 332).

➤ **Guideline 10.3   Distinguish between *random selection* and *random assignment*.**

When selecting individuals to participate in an experiment, it is desirable to select individuals at random. Whether or not the individuals were selected at random, it is desirable to assign the selected individuals at random to the comparison groups in an experiment. Consider Example 10.3.1, in which the researcher indicates that the selection was not random (i.e., children were referred—not selected at random) but that the assignment was at random (i.e., a randomized trial was used).

Example 10.3.1

Children were referred to the study by multiple community sources, including local school psychologists, principals, and a medical center. Children participated in a randomized, controlled trial of a cognitive-behavioral intervention....[3]

➤ **Guideline 10.4   For experiments with only one participant, describe the length of each condition.**

In some experiments, only one participant (or only one group of participants) is used. These are often referred to as *single-subject designs* (also called *behavior analysis*). In these, it is typical to observe the participant's behavior for a period before any treatments are administered (this is called the *baseline*), and then alternate treatments for varying periods. Example 10.4.1 illustrates how such an arrangement might be described, indicating the length of each condition, including the "reversal," which refers to returning to the original condition (i.e., without treatment).

Example 10.4.1

For baseline data, the infant's parents recorded the number of night awakenings for seven consecutive nights. On the next seven nights, the parents played the white noise machine [described above], while continuing to record the number of night awakenings. On the 15th and 16th nights, a reversal was instituted with the white noise machine turned off....

➤ **Guideline 10.5   Describe the experimental treatment in detail.**

Without a detailed description, readers will be unable to determine how to administer the treatment in order to get similar results.

In general, it is better to err on the side of providing too much detail than too little detail on experimental treatments. Examples 10.5.1 and 10.5.2 illustrate the degree of detail that might be expected by consumers of research.

---

[3] Wood (2006, p. 346).

Example 10.5.1

The stimuli were presented on a 21-inch color monitor. An IBM-compatible PC controlled stimulus presentation and response registration.... Stimuli were the digits 2 to 9 comprising a width of 1.24° visual angle and a height of 1.77° visual angle at a viewing distance of 127 cm. A circle and a square, both 1.43° in diameter, were used as cues. Cues and stimuli were presented in white color on a black background.[4]

Example 10.5.2

Participants logged on to the Web site, read a detailed description of the task and procedure, were asked to report their momentary affective state, and then were asked to set a goal for the first trial task. The Web page for goal setting gave participants the option to choose between nine different goal levels, ranging from 10% to 90% (e.g., "I want to perform better than 50% of the participants in this experiment"). After setting a goal for the first trial, participants were presented with the performance task and were given 5 min to work on the task. After submitting their task solutions, participants were presented with performance feedback. We provided half of the participants with accurate feedback by programming the electronic interface to provide relative performance feedback by comparing respondents' actual performance (computed as the number of correct solutions for the Remote Associates Test [RAT] and as the number of object/material uses provided by respondents for the brainstorming task; we describe these tasks below) with a distribution of responses constructed a priori. The other half received manipulated feedback that ranged between 35% and 80% (e.g., "For this trial, you have performed better than 35% of the participants"), which was randomized across trials for each participant. We used manipulated feedback to examine whether feedback has an effect on goal regulation....[5]

➢ Guideline 10.6 Describe physical controls over the administration of the experimental treatment.

This guideline is especially applicable to experiments in which colleagues and assistants are used to administer treatments. For instance, a researcher might have graduate students administer experimental counseling. Questions that should be addressed in such a situation are as follows: To what extent were the graduate students trained in the experimental counseling process? What type of supervision was provided for the graduate students? Were there spot-checks to determine if the graduate students were following protocol? Were the graduate students required to keep a log of their efforts to implement the counseling?

➢ Guideline 10.7 Describe the control condition.

Describe any conditions under which a control group was held. For instance, were the control group participants free to go their own way between

---

[4] Steinhauser & Hübner (2006, p. 520).
[5] Ilies & Judge (2005, p. 457).

before-and-after testing? Were they in the same classroom as the experimental students during the treatment of the experimental group? Were they assigned to do independent study? Varying conditions in the control condition could cause differences in how the control group responds, so the control condition should be described.

➤ Guideline 10.8 Describe steps taken to reduce the "expectancy effect."

When participants are able to determine (or guess) the expected effect of an experiment, they may respond accordingly (i.e., they may behave in the way they believe they are expected to respond). If any steps were taken to reduce this possibility, they should be described. Example 10.8.1 illustrates this guideline.

Example 10.8.1

While the purpose of the experiment was to examine students' attitudes toward professors of color (e.g., African Americans), the attitude scale touched on a number of issues relating to instruction in higher education in an effort to mask the true purpose of the experiment. Only the 10 items dealing with attitudes toward professors of color, however, were scored for the purposes of the analysis.

In pharmacological research, the *expectancy effect* is referred to as the *placebo effect*. It is standard procedure in experiments on new drugs to provide the control group with a *placebo* (an inert substance that looks like the experimental drug). To inhibit the expectancy effect, a *blind* procedure is typically used (i.e., the patient does not know whether the medication he or she is receiving is active or inert). In a *double-blind* procedure, neither the patient nor the individual dispensing the medication knows this. When a blind or double-blind procedure is used, it should be described, as illustrated in Example 10.8.2.

Example 10.8.2

A double-blind procedure was used in which neither the patient nor the nurse who was dispensing knew whether the active drug or the placebo was being dispensed.

➤ Guideline 10.9 If there was attrition, describe the dropouts.

This guideline refers to the attrition (i.e., dropping out) of individuals who began to participate in an experiment but dropped out before its conclusion. Attrition can make the interpretation of the results of an experiment difficult whenever there is the possibility that those who dropped out are different from those who remained, or those who dropped out of the experimental group are different from those who dropped out of the control group (called *differential attrition*).

For instance, in a study of an experimental drug, those who dropped out of the experimental group might have done so because they experienced serious side effects, leading the researchers to underestimate the side effects of the drug. One partial solution to this problem is to ask dropouts the reasons they dropped out. Unfortunately, sometimes dropouts cannot be located for questioning and some of those who are located may not be cooperative in providing such information.

Because attrition can be an important problem, the demographics and other available information about dropouts should be provided, if possible. Example 10.9.1 illustrates this guideline.

Example 10.9.1

Two boys (ages 10 and 11) and three girls (all age 10) dropped out of the experimental group because their families moved out of the school district. All five were Latino(a) and spoke English as a second language. Their percentile ranks on the *Metropolitan Reading Test* (English Version) ranged from 45 to 65, which is similar to the percentile ranks of the participants who did not drop out. None of the students in the control group dropped out.

In simple experiments (i.e., a treatment is given in a short amount of time with few demands on participants), there is likely to be little or no attrition, in which case this issue may not need to be addressed.

> ### Guideline 10.10   If participants were debriefed, mention it.

Debriefing consists of informing participants at the end of an experiment of its purposes and allowing participants to ask questions of the researchers. While informed consent forms provide general statements of purposes, debriefing describes the purposes in more detail. This process is described in Example 10.10.1. (cf., the last sentence).

Example 10.10.1

Each participant was provided adequate space to ensure confidentiality of responses and then provided with an informed consent form. The consent form described the study tasks (i.e., completing a set of short questionnaires and viewing various pictures), explained the need for frankness, and assured anonymity of responses. We then administered the study packets containing the stimuli and measures described above.... We concluded the session with presentation of a debriefing form stating the study's purposes and welcoming further contact with the researchers.[6]

Debriefing is especially important in experiments in which the specific purposes were not described in the consent form, which is often done to reduce the *expectancy effect* (see Guideline 10.8). Describing debriefing assures readers that participants' rights to knowledge of the full purposes of an experiment were protected.

---

[6] Corning, Krumm, & Smitham (2006, p. 342).

Exercise for Chapter 10

PART A

1. Should experimental procedures be described before *or* after measures?

2. Does the following statement describe "random selection" *or* "random assignment"?

   "From the entire population of 224 sixth graders, 50 were identified at random to participate in the experiment."

3. What is a baseline?

4. Should the length of a baseline be described?

5. Without a detailed description of the experimental treatment, readers will be unable to determine what?

6. Which guideline is especially applicable to experiments in which colleagues and assistants are used to administer treatments?

7. Is it ever desirable to describe the control condition?

8. Briefly define the *expectancy effect*.

9. What is the name of the problem that refers to individuals dropping out of an experiment?

PART B: Examine a report of an experiment published in a journal and answer the following questions.

10. If there was more than one group in the experiment, was the basis for assignment to groups clearly described? Explain.

11. Was the experimental treatment described in sufficient detail? Explain.

12. Was the topic of attrition addressed? If so, summarize what was said.

Chapter 11
Writing Analysis and Results Sections

While the Analysis subsection and the Results section typically are separate sections of a research report, they are closely aligned and are covered together in this chapter.

➤ **Guideline 11.1 "Analysis" is a subheading under the main heading of "Method."[1]**

A portion of Example 1.4.1 in Chapter 1 is reproduced below as Example 11.1.1 to show the placement of the material on Analysis (see the arrow in the example).

Example 11.1.1

Title in Upper- and Lowercase Letters
Abstract (a main heading; centered in bold)
A literature review that introduces the research problem (with no heading)
Method (a main heading; centered in bold)
Participants (a subheading; flush left in bold)
Measures (a subheading; flush left in bold)
Procedure (optional; a subheading; flush left in bold)
⇨**Analysis** (optional; a subheading; flush left in bold)

➤ **Guideline 11.2 The Analysis subsection is used sparingly in reports on quantitative research.**

If straightforward, widely recognized methods of statistical analysis were used to analyze the data, the subsection on analysis may be omitted in reports of quantitative research.

Quantitative researchers are likely to include a subsection on analysis if they have used advanced statistical methods that may not be familiar to their readers. Example 11.2.1 shows a portion of the Analysis subsection in which an advanced method is described. Notice in the example, the researcher (1) provides an explanation for the selection of the method of analysis and (2) cites a reference where more information on the method can be obtained, both of which are desirable characteristics.

---

[1] Some writers prefer to place the Analysis subheading immediately under the main heading of Results.

Example 11.2.1

The main analytic method employed here was censored regression with maximum likelihood estimation using LISREL 8.71 (Jöreskog & Sörbom, 1996). This regression approach was used because the distribution of the early adolescent delinquency scores was heavily influenced by zero values (55%), representing no delinquent behavior during the time window (for a discussion of the use of censored regression with crime measures, see Osgood, Finken, & McMorris, 2002).[2]

➢ Guideline 11.3 The Analysis subsection is usually included in reports on qualitative research.

Because there are many approaches to the analysis of qualitative data (e.g., transcripts from interviews), the approach selected for a particular research project should be named and briefly described, which is illustrated in Examples 11.3.1 and 11.3.2.—each of which is a portion of the subsection on analysis in a report on qualitative research. Notice that the researchers provide references where more information on the method of analysis can be obtained.

Example 11.3.1

Transcripts were analyzed using consensual qualitative research (CQR; Hill, Thompson, & Nutt Williams, 1997).... The research team adhered to the main CQR steps. First, they independently analyzed one transcript, assigning content either to a priori domains (rationally derived topics).... The team used these domains to independently code each transcript and met to discuss and reach consensus. On occasion throughout the coding process, the research team decided to add a domain in order to more clearly represent the data, resulting in five additional domains. After the 13 domains were identified, the team again independently reviewed each transcript and determined that each one reflected these domains.[3]

Example 11.3.2

Colaizzi's (1978) method of data analysis was used. The order of his steps is as follows: written protocols, significant statements, formulated meanings, clusters of themes, exhaustive description, and fundamental structure. It should be noted, however, that these steps do overlap. From each participant's description of the phenomenon, significant statements, which are phrases or sentences that directly describe the phenomenon, are extracted.... For each significant statement, the researcher formulates its meaning. Here, creative insight is called into play. Colaizzi cautioned that in this step of data analysis, the researcher must take a precarious leap from what the participants said to what they mean. Formulated meanings should never sever all connections from the original transcripts.... The next step entails organizing all the formulated meanings into clusters of themes. At this point, all the results to date are combined into an exhaustive description. This step

---

[2] Sullivan (2006, p. 299).
[3] Jacob & Veach (2005, p. 286).

is followed by revising the exhaustive description into a more condensed statement of the identification of the fundamental structure of the phenomenon being studied. The fundamental structure can be shared with the participants to validate how well it captured aspects of their experiences.[4]

➤ Guideline 11.4 "Results" is a main heading that follows the main heading "Method."

Portions of Examples 1.4.1 and 1.7.1 in Chapter 1 are reproduced below as Example 11.4.1 to show the placement of the results (see the arrow in the example).

Example 11.4.1

Title in Upper- and Lowercase Letters
Abstract (a main heading; centered in bold)
A literature review that introduces the research problem (with no heading)
Method (a main heading; centered in bold)
Participants (a subheading; flush left in bold)
Measures (a subheading; flush left in bold)
Procedure (optional; a subheading; flush left in bold)
Analysis (optional; a subheading; flush left in bold)
⇨**Results** (a main heading; centered in bold)

➤ Guideline 11.5 Organize the Results section around the research hypotheses, objectives, or questions.

This guideline helps readers understand the organization of the results. Example 11.5.1 shows the three research questions posed near the beginning of the report. It also shows a portion of the results. Notice how the results are organized around the three research questions.

Example 11.5.1

Research questions posed near the beginning of the report:

Specifically, three questions guided this research: (a) Is parental involvement associated with program effectiveness in terms of students' achievement? (b) Is parental involvement associated with attendance rates? and (c) Is parental involvement associated with their children's desire to continue to take part in the program?

Portions of the Results section, which illustrate the organization around the three research questions:

The first research question concerned the possible association between parental involvement and students' achievement. Table 1 shows the means and standard deviations on three achievement tests for two groups of students: students whose par-

---

[4] Beck & Watson (2010, p. 244)

ents were highly involved and students whose parents were less involved. A statistically significant difference was found between....

To examine the second research question, parents' scores on the involvement scale were correlated with their children's attendance in program sessions. Specifically, the involvement scores were correlated with number of days attended. This analysis indicated that parents' involvement was significantly correlated with....

The third research question concerned the association between parental involvement and children's desire to continue to take part in the program. The analysis of the data on this question revealed....

➤ Guideline 11.6 It is usually not necessary to show formulas or calculations in either the Analysis or Results sections.

Formulas and calculations for widely used statistics do not need to be shown in research reports. In addition, it is usually unnecessary to name the particular computer program used to perform the analysis.

➤ Guideline 11.7 The scores of individual participants usually are not shown.

Suppose a random sample of 50 students in an elementary school was tested with a standardized achievement test battery. Normally, a researcher would *not* list the scores of individual children. Instead, the researcher would provide summary statistics such as the mean and standard deviation. Note, however, that some instructors may require students who are writing term projects, theses, and dissertations to include participants' scores in an appendix so that the instructor can check the analysis.

➤ Guideline 11.8 Present descriptive statistics before inferential statistics.

For each set of scores, provide information on central tendency and variability (usually means and standard deviations), then present correlation coefficients, if any, and finally present the results of inferential statistical tests such as the *t* test.

For categorical (nominal) data, present frequencies and percentages before presenting the results of inferential statistical tests such as the chi-square test.

➤ Guideline 11.9 Organize large numbers of statistics in tables.

Tables are especially effective for helping readers compare groups. The table in Example 11.9.1 makes it easy to compare the ages of women and men.

Example 11.9.1

Table 1
Percentage and Number of Women and Men in Various Age Groups

Age	Women (*n* = 830)	Men (*n* = 723)
18 years and under	4.8% (*n* = 40)	8.7% (*n* = 63)
19–24 years	9.9% (*n* = 82)	13.3% (*n* = 96)
25–34 years	18.2% (*n* = 151)	25.4% (*n* = 184)
35–44 years	22.8% (*n* = 189)	19.4% (*n* = 140)
45–54 years	20.0% (*n* = 166)	15.4% (*n* = 111)
55–64 years	13.7% (*n* = 114)	13.8% (*n* = 100)
65–74 years	5.3% (*n* = 44)	2.6% (*n* = 19)
75 years and over	5.3% (*n* = 44)	1.4% (*n* = 10)
Total	100.0%	100.0%

➢ **Guideline 11.10   Give each table a number and caption (i.e., a descriptive title).**

In Example 11.9.1, the Table is numbered "Table 1" and has this caption: *Percentage and Number of Women and Men in Various Age Groups*.

Note that the captions should usually name the statistics presented in the table and the variables studied. Example 11.10.1 shows four titles that do this. For instance, in the first caption in this example, the statistics are number and percentage, while the variables are marital status and welfare status.

Example 11.10.1

Table 1   *Number and Percentage of Participants by Marital Status and Welfare Status*

Table 2   *Means and Standard Deviations on Reading and Mathematics*

Table 3   *Intercorrelation Matrix for Voting-Behavior Variables*

Table 4   *Analysis of Variance for Mathematics Scores*

When separate tables are presented for two or more groups, the title of each table should also name the group. Example 11.10.2 shows the titles of tables for two different groups.

Example 11.10.2

Table 1   *Intercorrelation Matrix of Middle-Level Managers' Personality Scores*

Table 2   *Intercorrelation Matrix of Chief Executive Officers' Personality Scores*

➤ **Guideline 11.11   Refer to statistical tables by number within the text of the Results section.**

Each statistical table included in a report should be referred to in the text by its number (e.g., "Table 1 presents the means and standard deviations for the adolescents."). Note that tables should usually be inserted in research reports *after* the first mention of them.[5]

➤ **Guideline 11.12   When describing the statistics presented in a table, point out only the highlights.**

Briefly describe the highlights of each table presented in the Results section. Because the values of the statistics are presented in a table, it is not necessary to repeat each value in the description of the results. This is illustrated in Example 11.12.1, which shows a statistical table, and Example 11.12.2, which shows the discussion of it. Note that in the discussion, only certain specific statistics are mentioned in order to assist the reader in getting an overview of the tabled results.

Example 11.12.1

Table 1

Percentage of Substance Use in Past Month of Urban and Suburban Samples

Grade	Drug A		Drug B		Drug C	
	Urban	Suburban	Urban	Suburban	Urban	Suburban
11	33.6	23.2	13.1	14.0	5.2	4.3
12	34.2	24.1	13.9	13.8	4.7	4.8

Example 11.12.2

Table 1 shows the percentage of urban and suburban 11th and 12th graders who reported using three illicit drugs during the previous month. Overall, Drug A had the highest percentages reporting its use, with percentages for subgroups ranging from 23.2% to 34.2%. Use of Drug B was reported by much smaller percentages of students (from 13.1% to 14.0% for subgroups). Use of Drug C was reported by relatively small percentages of students, with the highest percentage being 5.2% for urban 11th graders. Consistent with the hypothesis, the most striking difference between urban and suburban students was in the reported usage of Drug A, with higher percentages of urban students than suburban students reporting its use.

---

[5] In reports being submitted for publication, tables should be included at the end of the report so that the publisher can insert them at appropriate points when the reports are formatted for publication. Some instructors may prefer that students also do this in term-project research reports.

➤ Guideline 11.13 Statistical figures (e.g., drawings such as bar graphs) should be used sparingly.

Figures may be used to organize and describe data. They usually take up more space, however, than would a corresponding statistical table. Because space in journals is limited, figures should be used more sparingly than statistical tables. In term projects, theses, and dissertations, where space is not an issue, they may be used more frequently.

Because figures attract the eye better than tables, their best use is to present important data, especially striking data that might otherwise be overlooked in a table of statistical values. Example 11.13.1 shows such a figure, which illustrates a striking difference between the experimental groups and the control group on a scale from zero (no improvement) to 50 (outstanding improvement).

Like statistical tables, statistical figures should be numbered and given captions (titles) that name the variables and the statistics presented, which is done in the following example. Typically, figure numbers and titles are placed *below* the figures. For tables, they are placed *above*. Compare the placement of the caption in the table in Example 11.12.1 (i.e., *Percentage of Substance Use in...*) with the placement of the caption in the figure in Example 11.13.1 (i.e., Mean improvement scores for...).[6]

---

[6] Note that in American Psychological Association style, captions for tables are italicized, while captions for figures are not italicized.

Example 11.13.1

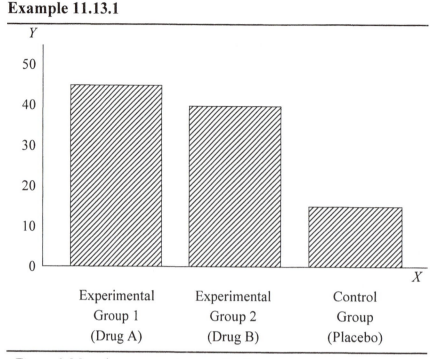

Figure 1. Mean improvement scores for three groups.

> ## ➢ Guideline 11.14   Statistical symbols should be underlined or italicized.

In Example 11.14.1, the statistical symbols (i.e., *t*, *df*, and *p*) are italicized. Without italics, "p" is just the letter "p." With italics, *p* is a statistical symbol that stands for *probability*.

Example 11.14.1

The mean of the experimental group was significantly higher than the mean of the control group ($t = 2.310$, $df = 10$, $p < .05$, two-tailed).

> ## ➢ Guideline 11.15   Use the proper case for each statistical symbol.

As statistical symbols, upper- and lowercase italicized letters often stand for entirely different statistics. For instance, a lowercase *f* stands for *frequency*, while an uppercase *F* is an inferential statistic used in significance testing. Also, a lowercase *t* is the symbol for a statistic frequently used to test the difference between two means, while an uppercase *T* is a special type of standardized test score.

For some statistics, the upper- and lowercases stand for the same statistic but communicate important information about sampling, in which the lowercase indicates that the value is an estimate based on a sample, while the uppercase indicates that the value is based on a population. For instance, researchers use *m* to stand for the mean (an average) based on a sample but use *M* to stand for the mean when it is based on a population. The same is true for the symbols for the standard deviation (*s* and *S*) and for the number of cases (*n* for the number in a sample and *N* for the number in a population).[7]

➤ Guideline 11.16   Consider when to spell out numbers.

Precise statistical values ordinarily should not be spelled out even if they are whole numbers. Thus, for instance, the number 8 should not be spelled out in a statement such as: "The median age was 8."

Note that numbers that start sentences should ordinarily be spelled out (e.g., Twenty-five students participated...). Also, whole numbers less than 10 within sentences should be spelled out (e.g., Of the five children who participated...).

➤ Guideline 11.17   Qualitative results should be organized and the organization made clear to the reader.

In qualitative studies, statistics are usually not reported. Instead, researchers report on major trends and themes that emerged from subjective and objective analyses of data such as transcribed interviews. The presentation of such results should be organized. To do this, consider using subheadings to guide the reader through the results. This is illustrated in Example 11.17.1, which is the first paragraph in the Results section of a report on a qualitative study. Note that it provides readers with a description of the organization of the results. The remaining portion of the results (not shown in the example) is divided into three parts with subheadings suggested in the example (e.g., Educational Aspirations of Parents and Youth).

Example 11.17.1

Key findings of the current study are divided into three sections. The first section addresses parents' educational and occupational aspirations, as well as those of their youth. The second section discusses parental knowledge of youth aspirations. The final section delineates the barriers to attainment of aspirations from parent and youth perspectives, and their input on what resources they needed to attain their aspirations.[8]

---

[7] Symbols used for the mean and standard deviation may vary among researchers. Because statistics textbooks often use X-bar (an X with a bar over it) as the symbol for the mean, a small percentage of researchers use it instead of *m* or *M* in their research reports. In addition, some researchers prefer to use *sd* and *SD* instead of *s* or *S* as the symbol for the standard deviation.

[8] Behnke, Piercy, & Diversi (2004, pp. 21–22).

See Chapter 14 for additional information on reporting the results of qualitative research.

Exercise for Chapter 11

PART A

1. According to this chapter, is the Analysis subsection more likely to appear in reports of "quantitative research" *or* in reports of "qualitative research"?

2. Is Results a "subheading" *or* a "main heading"?

3. "In the Results section, it is important to show all formulas and calculations." Is this statement true *or* false?

4. Should "descriptive statistics" *or* "inferential statistics" be presented first?

5. The captions for tables should usually name what two things?

6. Should all the values in statistical tables be mentioned in the narrative of the Results section? Explain.

7. According to this chapter, are "statistical tables" *or* "statistical figures" more common in research reports published in journals?

8. How does "p" differ from *p* in terms of their meanings?

9. How does *n* differ from *N* in terms of their meanings?

10. What is wrong in the following statement?

   "Initially, there were 60 children in the control group. 15 of these children dropped out of the study."

PART B

11. Examine the Results sections of a quantitative research report published in a journal. List the guidelines in this chapter that were followed by the researcher. Be prepared to discuss your findings in class.

12. Locate a statistical table in a published article that you think has a good title (i.e., caption). Copy it, and bring it to class for discussion.

Notes

Chapter 12
Writing Discussion Sections

This chapter presents guidelines for writing the last section of a research report in a journal article or the last chapter of a thesis or dissertation, which typically begins with one of various headings such as "Summary and Discussion," "Discussion and Conclusions," "Conclusions and Implications," or simply "Discussion."

➤ Guideline 12.1 "Discussion" is a main heading that follows the main heading "Results."

Example 12.1.1 shows the placement of the Discussion section relative to the other parts of a research report discussed up to this point in this book (see the arrow in the example).

Example 12.1.1

Title in Upper- and Lowercase Letters
Abstract (a main heading; centered in bold)
A literature review that introduces the research problem (with no heading)
Method (a main heading; centered in bold)
Participants (a subheading; flush left in bold)
Measures (a subheading; flush left in bold)
Procedure (optional; a subheading; flush left in bold)
Analysis (optional; a subheading; flush left in bold)
Results (a main heading; centered in bold)
⇨**Discussion** (a main heading; centered in bold)

➤ Guideline 12.2 Consider starting the Discussion with a summary.

Authors of long research reports, theses, and dissertations often begin their Discussion sections with a summary of the highlights of the material that preceded it. For short reports, a summary is usually not necessary.

➤ Guideline 12.3 Early in the Discussion section, refer to the research hypotheses, objectives, or questions.

Briefly restate the hypotheses, objectives, or questions and indicate whether the data support the hypotheses, whether the research objectives were achieved, or what answers were obtained for the research questions.

This is illustrated in Example 12.3.1, which is the beginning of the Discussion section.

Example 12.3.1

The primary purpose of the present research was to identify and distinguish particular risk factors that contribute to alcohol use, symptoms of alcohol use disorder, and antisocial behavior in a sample of adolescent and young adult students attending a GED program.[1]

Following this guideline helps to refocus readers' attention on the fundamental purposes of the research report and sets the stage for other aspects of the discussion.

➢ Guideline 12.4   Point out whether results of the current study are consistent with the literature described in the literature review.

Because the review of the literature near the beginning of a research report helps set the stage for the current study, it is important to discuss at the end how the current findings relate to those reported earlier in the literature review.

Examples 12.4.1 and 12.4.2 illustrate this guideline.

Example 12.4.1

Overall, several of our findings were consistent with prior research. First, Catholic school students experienced larger math gains from 10th through 12th grade than comparable public school students. This finding is consistent with research from both HS&B and NELS:88 (Bryk et al., 1993; Gamoran, 1996; Hoffer, 1998; Hoffer et al., 1985). Thus, changes in the Catholic and public sectors have not eliminated the Catholic advantage in high school achievement; it is now observable over a 20-year period beginning in the 1980s through the early 2000s.[2]

Example 12.4.2

A significant proportion of normal-weight men felt they were underweight, and an even larger percentage of overweight men thought they were normal weight. The opposite emerged for women: A large number of normal-weight women felt they were overweight. These findings support those from research with adolescents and university students, suggesting that weight misperceptions evident in early through late adolescence are also found in adults.[3]

---

[1] Owens & Bergman (2010, p. 90).
[2] Carbonaro & Covay (2010, p. 175).
[3] McCreary & Sadava (2001, p. 113).

➢ Guideline 12.5 Consider interpreting the results and offering explanations for them in the Discussion section.

Following this guideline helps readers understand the results and put them in context. Because interpretations and explanations go beyond the data actually collected, researchers should be careful not to imply that they are data-based explanations. Instead, they are possible explanations that are consistent with the data. The authors of Example 12.5.1 offer an explanation of their findings.

Example 12.5.1

It is interesting to speculate on possible reasons why the fear levels expressed by the 10-year-old children were so much greater than those expressed by the 8-year-old children in this study. One possibility is that the younger children did not have the conceptual background to fully understand the presentation made in the experimental setting. Specifically, they might have....

It is especially desirable to offer possible explanations for unexpected findings. In Example 12.5.2, the researchers offer an explanation for the finding that Latina mothers' support was associated only with their daughters' academic motivation, while Latino fathers' support was associated only with their sons' motivation.

Example 12.5.2

A possible explanation for this unexpected finding comes from research that has found that mothers are more likely to spend time with their daughters and fathers are more likely to spend time with their sons.... This may be especially true in Latino populations, as researchers have documented that parents are more likely to engage in gender role socialization with same-sex adolescents....[4]

➢ Guideline 12.6 Mention important strengths and limitations in the Discussion section.

Strengths and limitations of the research methodology are sometimes first mentioned in the introduction or the section on methods. Because strengths and limitations can affect the interpretations of data covered in the Discussion section, it is usually appropriate to mention the most important ones in the Discussion. The authors of Example 12.6.1 point out some strengths of their study. By pointing out that a study is especially strong methodologically, researchers encourage their readers to give more credence to their study, which is especially important if there are conflicting conclusions reached in weaker studies.

---

[4] Alfaro, Umaña-Taylor, & Bámaca (2006, p. 288).

Example 12.6.1

The current study has several strengths. It collected information on IPV [intimate partner violence] from both partners, which enhances the probability of identification of spousal violence.... [In addition,] interviews with Hispanics were conducted in English or Spanish, which allows for inclusion of bilingual and monolingual respondents. [Third,] the longitudinal design allows for the assessment of incidence and recurrence of violence.[5]

Example 12.6.2 shows a statement regarding the limitations of a study. A frank discussion of limitations helps warn readers to be cautious in drawing conclusions from a study.

Example 12.6.2

Although this research contributes preliminary insight to assist schools when creating antibullying programs, it is not without limitations. The most obvious of which is the use of self-report, which may or may not be an accurate description of how students act in real social situations.[6]

Students who are writing theses and dissertations should provide detailed descriptions of the limitations of their research. Such statements will help to reassure their committee members that the students are knowledgeable of important methodological issues in their research. Students who are writing research reports as term projects should determine how detailed their professors want their discussions of limitations to be.

See Chapter 8 for an additional discussion of writing strengths and limitations.

➤ **Guideline 12.7   It is usually inappropriate to introduce new data or new references in the Discussion section.**

The Discussion section of a research report should be used to summarize and interpret what was presented earlier. The introduction of new data or references distracts from this purpose.

➤ **Guideline 12.8   When possible, state specific implications in the Discussion section.**

The implications of a study are usually stated in the form of actions that individuals or organizations should take based on the results of the study. This is illustrated in Examples 12.8.1 and 12.8.2.

---

[5] Caetano, Ramisetty-Mikler, & McGrath (2004, p. 75).
[6] Russell, Kraus, & Ceccherini (2010, pp. 265–266).

Example 12.8.1

The large effects observed here hint at promising educational interventions. These interventions would provide students with external support by providing physical or visual access to objects described by a story followed by instructing the learner to imagine story events. By familiarizing students with story characters and settings before and during a narrative in this manner, it is expected students' understanding and recall of story events will improve.[7]

Example 12.8.2

The applications of the program should be further examined by including an older adult population or even more frail elders with various functional dependency levels. The SY [Silver Yoga] program could be incorporated as an exercise activity in assisted living facilities or other long-term care facilities to promote physical fitness of institutional elders. The directors of the facilities could recruit volunteers to learn the program and lead the elders to practice in groups in the facilities regularly. It is essential that more exercise-based activities with evidence-based outcomes be incorporated into long-term care facilities to enhance elders' physical fitness and to document health in elders.[8]

In the discussion of the results of pilot studies, researchers often hedge in their statements of implications by beginning them with a caution such as the one shown in Example 12.8.3.

Example 12.8.3

If the results obtained in this pilot study are confirmed in more definitive studies, the following implications should be considered by....

➢ Guideline 12.9   Be specific when making recommendations for future research.

It is uninformative to end a research report with a vague statement such as "Further research is needed." Instead, researchers should point out what specific directions this research might take in order to advance knowledge of a topic. Examples 12.9.1 and 12.9.2 illustrate the degree of specificity often found in research reports published in journal articles.

Example 12.9.1

Another interesting avenue for future research is to examine the morale and productivity of employees who do not use drugs at work. Most research has been concerned with the work outcomes of the person using drugs. However, because this study shows that workplace substance use may be prevalent in certain segments of the workforce, it would be useful to see whether exposure to individuals who use drugs at work or arrive at work impaired has a negative impact on the morale and

---

[7] Marley, Levin, & Glenberg (2010, p. 412).
[8] Chen, Fan, Wang, Wu, Li, & Lin (2010, p. 370).

performance of coworkers who do not use drugs at work or come to work impaired. If it does, the impact of workplace drug use on productivity may be broader than what is typically assumed.[9]

Example 12.9.2

The results of this study suggest a number of future directions for research aimed at understanding the relation between depression, suicide, and sleep disturbances. In particular, future research should examine whether disturbing dreams and nightmares are associated with depression and suicidality via disruptions in sleep quality or via content that increases negative cognitions and emotional dysregulation. This research should aim to determine whether experiences of disturbing dreams or nightmares serve to increase insomnia or decrease sleep quality overall. Finally, the relation between these sleep disturbances and....[10]

Note that students who are writing a thesis or dissertation might be expected to discuss suggestions for future research in more detail than shown in Examples 12.9.1 and 12.9.2.

> ### Guideline 12.10   Consider using subheadings within the Discussion section.

In a long Discussion section, subheadings can help readers follow the discussion. Example 12.10.1 shows some subheadings that might be used.

Example 12.10.1

Discussion (a main heading; centered in bold)
Summary (optional; a subheading; flush left in bold)
Strengths of the Current Study (optional; a subheading; flush left in bold)
Limitations (optional; a subheading; flush left in bold)
Implications (optional; a subheading; flush left in bold)
Directions for Future Research (optional; a subheading; flush left in bold)

Exercise for Chapter 12

PART A

1. Is Discussion a "main heading" *or* a "subheading"?

2. According to this chapter, should a Discussion always begin with a summary? Explain.

---

[9] Frone (2006, p. 868).
[10] Cukrowicz et al. (2006, p. 9).

3. "Research hypotheses, objectives, and questions should never be repeated in the Discussion section." Is this statement true *or* false?

4. Should writers refer to the literature cited at the beginning of their reports in their Discussion sections? Why? Why not?

5. Is it acceptable for researchers to offer explanations for their results that go beyond the data actually analyzed?

6. Is it usually appropriate to introduce new references in the Discussion section of a research report?

7. Is it appropriate for researchers to describe possible implications of their results, *or* should they just restrict themselves to an objective discussion of the actual data?

8. According to this chapter, is it appropriate to end a research report with only this sentence: "Further research is needed."? Explain.

PART B

9. Read a research article published in a journal, thesis, or dissertation, and examine the Discussion section to answer the following questions.

   A. Does the researcher discuss the consistency of the results with previously published results?
   B. Does the researcher mention important strengths and limitations of the current study?
   C. Does the researcher explicitly state the implications of the results?
   D. Does the researcher use subheadings under the main heading of Discussion? If yes, what subheadings were used?

Notes

Chapter 13
Writing Abstracts

An *abstract* is a summary of the report. It is placed below the title in a journal article. In a thesis or dissertation, it is usually placed on a separate page following the title page.

➤ Guideline 13.1   Determine the maximum length permissible for an abstract.

For journals, abstracts are often limited to 250 words or fewer. For theses, dissertations, and term projects, the word limit may be more generous. In either case, an abstract should be short enough to allow readers to conduct a quick read to determine if the research report will be of interest to them.

➤ Guideline 13.2   If space permits, consider beginning an abstract by describing the general problem area.

Researchers often begin their abstracts with a brief statement regarding the importance of the problem area. Example 13.2.1 shows the beginning of an abstract that follows this guideline.

Example 13.2.1

Contrary to the "model minority" myth, growing research indicates that the rates of mental health problems among Asian Americans may be higher than was initially assumed....[1]

➤ Guideline 13.3   If space is limited, consider beginning by summarizing the research hypotheses, objectives, or questions.

When space is limited, it is best to begin with a statement (or summary) of the research hypotheses, objectives, or questions. Examples 13.3.1 and 13.3.2 show the first sentences of abstracts that follow this guideline.

Example 13.3.1

The aim of this study was to develop and validate the Disordered Eating Attitude Scale to measure disordered eating attitudes, defined as abnormal beliefs, thoughts, feelings, behaviors, and relationship regarding food.[2]

---

[1] Iwamoto, Liao, & Liu (2010, p. 15).
[2] Alvarenga, Scagliusi, & Philippi (2010, p. 379).

Example 13.3.2

The purpose of this study was to investigate how education majors' images of teaching, teachers, and children change before and after student teaching, with special attention to the grade level (Grades 1–2, 3–4, 5–6) taught by the student teachers at primary school in Japan.[3]

Many researchers indicate their purpose without using the terms *hypothesis*, *objective*, *purpose*, or *question*, which is acceptable. For instance, Example 13.3.3 shows the first sentence of an abstract. It is clear from the sentence that the objective of the study was to evaluate the impact of social skills training.

Example 13.3.3

This study is an investigation of whether social skills training provided by paraprofessionals to elementary grade children with Autism Spectrum Disorders (ASD) in both partially and fully included classrooms can result in perceived gains in social skills as measured by teacher ratings.[4]

➤ Guideline 13.4   Highlights of the methodology should be summarized.

Information on methodology (such as how variables were measured or what treatments were given in an experiment) helps potential readers determine whether the report will be of interest to them.

Example 13.4.1 shows the beginning of an abstract. Notice that the first sentence describes the purpose, while the second and third sentences summarize the research methods used.

Example 13.4.1

The aim of this study was to evaluate a standard 10-minute peer education protocol to reduce binge drinking among Dutch adolescents at campsites during summer holidays. Using a quasi-experimental design, we evaluated the effects of the peer education protocol as applied by trained peer educators. We collected data by telephone interviews 14 days after the holiday.[5]

➤ Guideline 13.5   Highlights of the results should be included.

Example 13.5.1 shows a complete abstract. Notice that the abstract starts with the research purpose. Next, it summarizes the research methods. Then, there is a summary of the results. This arrangement is recommended for a short abstract.

---

[3] Mishima, Horimoto, & Mori (2010, p. 769).
[4] Mazurik-Charles & Stefanou (2010, p. 161).
[5] Planken & Boer (2010, p. 35).

Example 13.5.1

The purpose of this study was to assess whether reaction time in persons with intellectual disabilities can be improved with an exercise program. Fifty children and adolescents (M age = 14.7 yr., SD = 1.4, range = 11–18) with mild intellectual disability without Downs syndrome were randomly divided into control (20 boys, 5 girls) and experimental (19 boys, 6 girls) groups. The experimental group participated in a structured physical fitness program for 12 weeks. Reaction time was assessed at baseline and after 12 weeks. Significant improvements in reaction time were observed in the exercise group but not for the control group. Results indicated that reaction time can be improved with an exercise program in youth with intellectual disability.[6]

➤ Guideline 13.6 Point out any unexpected results.

Unexpected results can lead to advancement of knowledge by stimulating further research to help understand such results. Thus, unexpected results should be pointed out in an abstract, as illustrated in Example 13.6.1 (italics have been added for emphasis).

Example 13.6.1

The present research examined the influence of improved knowledge of odds and mathematical expectation on the gambling behavior of university students. A group of 198 students in an introductory statistics class received instruction on probability theory using examples from gambling. A comparison group of 134 students received generic instruction on probability, and another group of 138 students in classes on unrelated topics received no mathematical instruction. Students receiving the intervention demonstrated superior ability to calculate gambling odds as well as resistance to gambling fallacies 6 months after the intervention. *Unexpectedly, this improvement in knowledge and skill was not associated with any decreases in actual gambling behavior.* The implication of this research is that enhanced mathematical knowledge on its own may be insufficient to change gambling behavior.[7]

➤ Guideline 13.7 If a study is strongly tied to a theory, name the theory in the abstract.

Typically, theories provide principles that help explain a wide variety of observations. For instance, social learning theory applies to a large number of phenomena observed in teaching and learning studies.

When the results of individual studies are consistent with predictions based on a theory, they lend support to the theory. On the other hand, when

---

[6] Yildirim, Erbahçecí, Ergun, Pitetti, & Beets (2010, p. 178).
[7] Williams & Connolly (2006, p. 62).

results of individual studies are inconsistent with a theory, that theory, or at least portions of it, might need to be reconsidered.

Because of the importance of theories in advancing knowledge, they are sometimes mentioned in the titles of research articles. More often, they are mentioned in the abstracts. Examples 13.7.1 and 13.7.2 show complete abstracts and illustrate how to follow this guideline.

Example 13.7.1

Socioemotional selectivity theory (SST) posits that emotionally close relationships are increasingly valued as people perceive constraints on time. Based on SST, this study of 1,532 older married persons hypothesized that emotional dimensions of marriage would more strongly predict adjustment at higher levels of functional disability. High levels of marital closeness were negatively associated with depression and anxiety and positively associated with self-esteem. Consistent with predictions derived from SST, marital closeness moderated the negative psychological effects of high levels of functional disability on depression, anxiety, and self-esteem. Results are discussed in the context of SST and traditional stress-buffering models of social support.[8]

Example 13.7.2

Nonadherence in the management of chronic illness is a pervasive clinical challenge. Although researchers have identified multiple correlates of adherence, the field remains relatively atheoretical. The authors propose a cognitive-affective model of medication adherence based on social support theory and research. Structural equation modeling of longitudinal survey data from 136 mainly African American and Puerto Rican men and women with HIV/AIDS provided preliminary support for a modified model. Specifically, baseline data indicated social support was associated with less negative affect and greater spirituality, which, in turn, were associated with self-efficacy to adhere. Self-efficacy to adhere at baseline predicted self-reported adherence at 3 months, which predicted chart-extracted viral load at 6 months. The findings have relevance for theory building, intervention development, and clinical practice.[9]

➤ Guideline 13.8   Mention any unique aspects of a study.

Elements that make a research study unique usually should be mentioned in an abstract. For instance, if a study is the first true experiment (i.e., an experiment with randomization) on a particular problem, this unique aspect should be pointed out in the abstract.

---

[8] Mancini & Bonanno (2006, p. 600).
[9] Simoni, Frick, & Huang (2006, p. 74).

➤ Guideline 13.9   Mention if a line of inquiry is new.

Individuals often review abstracts to identify new ways of working with problems. If the line of inquiry is new, its newness should be pointed out in an abstract, as illustrated in Example 13.9.1 (italics added for emphasis).

Example 13.9.1

A major focus of school nursing interventions is to improve school attendance. In many schools, parents are required to leave work and/or to arrange transportation to bring their children over-the-counter medicines. Many times these children went home, missing class and making it difficult to keep up with classwork. The purpose of this study was to examine the impact of a *new policy and procedure* allowing school nurses to administer certain over-the-counter medications in elementary schools in a southern New Mexico public school district. "Sent home" rates before implementation of the new policy were compared with sent home rates for 2 years following implementation. Although not statistically significant, findings indicated that over-the-counter medication administration by school nurses does show a trend toward sending fewer students home and, therefore, keeping them in the learning environment.[10]

➤ Guideline 13.10   If implications and suggestions for future research are emphasized in the report, consider concluding the abstract by mentioning them.

This guideline applies when the Discussion section of a report describes important implications and/or explicit suggestions for future research. In contrast, if these elements are mentioned only in passing, they should not be mentioned in an abstract.

Notice the last sentence in the abstract in Example 13.6.1, which refers to implications.

➤ Guideline 13.11   An abstract should usually be short; however, there are exceptions.

Many journals limit the number of words that may be included in abstracts—some as short as 250 or fewer. For instance, journals published by the American Psychological Association limit abstracts to a maximum of 150 to 250 words, depending on the particular journal. Example 13.11.1 shows the suggested organization for a short abstract.

---

[10] Foster & Keele (2006, p. 108).

Example 13.11.1

Suggested elements to cover in a short abstract (no subheadings):

1. Research hypotheses, purposes, or questions. These may need to be abbreviated or summarized if they are extensive.
2. Highlights of the research methods.
3. Highlights of the results.

Students who are writing theses and dissertations should determine their institution's requirements regarding length and number of words. When long abstracts are permitted (or required), consider incorporating information on the importance of the problem and the implications of the results in addition to the other elements mentioned in the earlier guidelines in this chapter. In a long abstract, subheadings such as those shown in Example 13.11.2 might be used.

Example 13.11.2

Suggested elements to cover in a long abstract:

1. Background
   (Describe the problem area and its importance.)
2. Research Hypotheses
   (or Research Purposes or Research Questions)
3. Method
4. Results
5. Implications
6. Suggestions for Further Research

The amount of emphasis to put on each element in an abstract is a subjective matter. When writing it, keep in mind that the goal is to provide enough information for potential readers to make informed decisions on whether to read the entire research report.

➤ **Guideline 13.12   Consider using subheadings in an abstract.**

Some journals require the use of subheadings, even in short abstracts. Subheadings may also be included in theses, dissertations, and term projects. Example 13.12.1 shows a short abstract with subheadings (with the subheadings in bold for emphasis).

Example 13.12.1

Objective: The purpose of this study was to determine the efficacy of 24 weeks of the senior-tailored silver yoga (SY) exercise program for transitional frail elders. **Methods:** A convenience sample of 69 elders in assisted living facilities were assigned randomly to the SY group ($n = 38$) or to the control group ($n = 31$) on the basis of the facilities where they resided, and 55 of them completed this quasi-experimental pretest and posttest study. Intervention was conducted three times per week, 70 minutes per session, for 24 weeks. Physical fitness (body composition, cardiovascular-respiratory functions, body flexibility, muscle power, endurance, balance, and agility) were examined at baseline, at 12 weeks, and at the end of the 24th week of the study. **Results**: At the end of the study, the physical fitness indicators of participants in the SY group had improved significantly, and they had better physical fitness than participants in the control group (all p values < .05). **Discussion:** It was recommended that the SY exercises be incorporated as an activity program in assisted living facilities to promote the physical fitness of transitional frail elders.[11]

Exercise for Chapter 13

PART A

1. According to this chapter, with what should an abstract begin if space is limited?

2. In light of this chapter, would you expect to find highlights of the research methodology described in an abstract?

3. Should highlights of the results be included in an abstract?

4. Is it desirable to point out unexpected results in an abstract?

5. If a study is strongly tied to a theory, should the theory be named in the abstract?

6. Are there any major deficiencies in the following abstract? Explain.

   Abstract: Two hundred second-grade students were administered a battery of published cognitive tests that measured a variety of academic achievement variables. The students were drawn from three elementary schools in a large, urban school district. All were tested near the end of second grade. Test administrators administered the tests in three sessions because students might become fatigued by taking the entire battery in a single testing session. The three research hypotheses were confirmed. Implications for cognitive development and directions for future research are discussed.

---

[11] Chen, Fan, Wang, Wu, Li, & Lin (2010, p. 364).

PART B: Locate an abstract for a research report published in a journal that you believe illustrates a majority of the guidelines in this chapter. Bring a copy to class for discussion.

Chapter 14

A Closer Look at Writing Reports of Qualitative Research

With certain obvious exceptions, such as some of the guidelines on reporting statistical results, the guidelines in the previous chapters should be considered when writing reports of qualitative research. This chapter presents guidelines that are specific to reporting qualitative research.

> ➢ **Guideline 14.1 Consider using the term *qualitative* in the title of the report.**

Because the vast majority of research in the social and behavioral sciences continues to be quantitative, using the term qualitative in a title helps interested readers locate qualitative research. Examples 14.1.1 and 14.1.2 show how some researchers have used the term in titles.

Example 14.1.1

Patients' Perceptions of Joint Teleconsultations: A Qualitative Evaluation[1]

Example 14.1.2

Adolescents' Perception of Risk and Challenge: A Qualitative Study[2]

Notice that in both the above titles, the term qualitative was used in the subtitles instead of the main titles. This is appropriate because most readers searching for research reports are probably more interested in the variables studied (e.g., perceptions of joint teleconsultations) than in the methodological approach (e.g., a qualitative study).

> ➢ **Guideline 14.2 Consider using the term *qualitative* in the abstract of the report.**

If space does not permit mention of the qualitative nature of a study in its title, consider mentioning it in the abstract, as illustrated in Example 14.2.1 (italics added for emphasis).

---

[1] Harrison, MacFarlane, Murray, & Wallace (2006, p. 81).
[2] Rodham, Brewer, Mistral, & Stallard (2006, p. 261).

Example 14.2.1

This article describes a *qualitative study* that explored the perceptions of graduating students from a northeast baccalaureate nursing program regarding their life experiences with cultural diversity. Thirteen students were interviewed using an interview guide, and interviews were recorded on audiotape. Information obtained included participants' cultural heritage, life experiences before entering a nursing program, educational and clinical experiences in the nursing program, knowledge about cultural competence, and the students' reflections on their ability to provide culturally competent care. Primarily *qualitative methods* were used to gather and analyze data. This article focuses on one of the major themes that emerged: defining life experiences related to cultural diversity. Data were reanalyzed focusing on this theme, and three life patterns emerged: positive, neutral, and conflicted. These patterns affected the students' interest and desire to provide culturally competent care. Implications for further research and nursing education are discussed.[3]

Guidelines 14.1 and 14.2 are especially important when qualitative research has been conducted on a topic that has traditionally been approached quantitatively. The use of qualitative methodology on such a topic is a distinguishing characteristic of the research.

➢ Guideline 14.3   Consider discussing the choice of qualitative over quantitative methodology.

A discussion of the choice of qualitative over quantitative methodology is usually placed in the introduction of a research report or in the section on methods. This guideline is especially recommended when writing research for an audience that is quantitatively oriented, such as readers of a journal that usually publishes quantitative research.

Example 14.3.1 illustrates this guideline. The researchers who wrote it were interested in gaining a better understanding of the lives of preadolescent foster children. The stories that the researchers analyzed were stories the children told in interviews about their lives.

Example 14.3.1

Qualitative approaches are particularly suited to examining the stories of children. Stories reflect a social contextualization of ideas and contain rich content that does not lend itself well to traditional quantitative approaches.... Interviewing children gives this "socially silenced group...[whose] opinions are not heard in the public sphere" an opportunity to have a voice....[4]

---

[3] Reeves & Fogg (2006, p. 171).
[4] Whiting & Lee (2003, p. 289).

➤ Guideline 14.4 Consider "revealing yourself" to the readers.

While quantitative researchers are taught to be *objective* and distance themselves from their research participants to avoid influencing the outcome, qualitative researchers recognize the inherently subjective nature of research. In addition, most qualitative researchers use methods that involve direct interactions between researchers and their participants such as in-depth interviews, participant observation, and focus groups. Because of the interactive nature of much qualitative research, some researchers consider it appropriate to describe themselves when the descriptions may be relevant to what is being studied. An appropriate place to do this is in the Analysis subsection of the main section on methods (see the arrow in Example 11.1.1 in Chapter 11).

The researchers who wrote Example 14.4.1 "revealed themselves" in the report on a study of the coping responses of Asian, Black, and Latino/Latina New York City residents following the attack on September 11, 2001.

Example 14.4.1

The judges/researchers for this study were two African American female counseling psychologists. One of the investigators had expertise in the CQR [consensual qualitative research] method, and the other had limited experience with this type of methodology. Moreover, the judges had extensive experience in counseling Asian, Black, and Latino/Latina individuals in the United States, and were proficient in the areas of coping and problem-solving appraisal among the populations of interest.[5]

➤ Guideline 14.5 Avoid calling a sample *purposive* if it is actually a sample of convenience.

A *purposive sample* is one that a researcher believes to be especially well suited for obtaining meaningful data on a particular research problem. In other words, it consists of participants that a researcher deliberately selects because they have characteristics that make them especially worthy of attention.

When researchers use participants who are selected simply because they are convenient (such as students who happen to be enrolled in a professor's psychology course), the sample should be identified as one of convenience—not purposive—by using a phrase such as "a sample of convenience" or "accidental sample." This is illustrated in Example 14.5.1.

---

[5] Constantine, Alleyne, Caldwell, McRae, & Suzuki (2006, p. 296).

Example 14.5.1

We obtained a convenience sample of 10 families by inviting youth and families from a local Latino after-school program to participate in the study.[6]

➢ Guideline 14.6   If a purposive sample was used, state the basis for selection of participants.

In Example 14.6.1, the researchers purposefully selected cases at the extreme of a distribution.

Example 14.6.1

Because we were interested in exploring factors that support involvement in extracurricular activities, we selected a purposive sample of the most highly involved and competent individuals in childhood to interview about their decisions when they reached adolescence. This sampling procedure is in accordance with Patton's (1990) recommendation for qualitative researchers to purposefully select cases at the extremes of a distribution because they are more likely to contain rich information. Moreover, other scholars have suggested this sampling procedure when examining understudied populations....[7]

➢ Guideline 14.7   Describe how participants were recruited.

Whether a sample of convenience or a purposive sample was used, readers are likely to be interested in how the participants were recruited. This is especially true when studying potentially sensitive issues because poor recruitment procedures may lead to highly atypical samples. Example 14.7.1 shows a description of the recruitment of African American men. Note that the researchers used a variety of recruitment procedures in a variety of geographical locations, which would be expected to result in a diverse sample. Also, note that despite these efforts, the researchers still characterize the sample as being a convenience sample.

Example 14.7.1

The data for this project were collected from a convenience sample of men residing in the following metropolitan areas: Michigan, Georgia, Maryland, New York, and Virginia. Consistent with the principles of community-based research..., knowledgeable African American community residents (including research assistants associated with this project) actively participated in the recruitment process. Recruiters for the present study distributed and collected survey materials. Participants were recruited through public announcements, e-mail, fliers, and word of mouth. Surveys were also distributed in local businesses, barbershops, and on the campus of historically African American and predominantly European American

---

[6] Behnke, Piercy, & Diversi (2004, p. 19).
[7] Fredricks et al. (2002, p. 72).

college campuses. The initial data collection resulted in a snowball effect. In other words, as men completed the survey, some volunteered to distribute surveys to other men, whereas others offered to encourage other men to participate in the study. [8]

➢ Guideline 14.8 Provide demographic information.

Demographics (i.e., background variables) help readers "see" the participants. Even though qualitative researchers avoid statistics in the reporting of results, when describing the demographics of participants, statistics can be useful. This is illustrated in Example 14.8.1.

Example 14.8.1

This study included American and Dutch participants. The American focus group participants consisted of 48 independently living older adults (29 women and 19 men) in the age range from 65 to 80 ($M = 71.2$, $SD = 4.9$). The sample was ethnically diverse; 25% were African American, 10% Hispanic, and 65% Caucasian.... The Dutch participants consisted of 20 independently living older adults in the age range from 65 to 80 years ($M = 71.1$, $SD = 3.9$), 9 women and 11 men, 80% Caucasian and 20% of other ethnic origins (one person came from Spain, one from Surinam, and two from Indonesia).[9]

➢ Guideline 14.9 Provide specific information on data collection methods.

In an interview study, it is insufficient to state merely that "in-depth, semistructured interviews were conducted." Readers will want to know how the initial questions were developed as well as the topics these questions were designed to cover. Example 14.9.1 illustrates this.

Example 14.9.1

An interview format was selected due to the depth of data it can offer and its ability to reveal participants' own perspectives on their experiences. The semistructured nature of the interview protocol allowed for exploratory probing and further questioning when necessary. The interview questions explored family functioning, reasons for immigration, and experiences in the United States, especially with regard to school, family, and peers. There were also questions about mental health concerns and coping as related to immigration.

The interview protocol was developed after performing an extensive review of the literature. The questions were primarily based on the research on cultural adjustment (Rosenthal & Feldman, 1990, 1996; Padilla et al., 1985) and acculturation.... Questions were designed specifically for Asian immigrant youth.

---

[8] Hammond & Mattis (2005, p. 117).
[9] Melenhorst, Rogers, & Bouwhuis (2006, p. 191).

Interviewers were encouraged to probe further if there were any ambiguities in participants' responses.[10]

Note that it may not be necessary to state the actual questions used, especially if the wording of the questions varied somewhat from participant to participant and the content of the questions changed over the course of a qualitative study in light of the data collected from earlier participants. On the other hand, if there were key questions that were asked of all participants, consider including them in the research report. If there were many questions, either provide just a sample for each domain of interest or provide them all in a table or appendix.

In Example 14.9.2, the researchers describe the areas covered by the questions and then refer the readers to a table that contains 17 key questions (e.g., "Will you tell me about a time when your child had difficulty breathing during the night?") organized under six topics (e.g., "Family response to asthma"). Also, note these desirable characteristics of Example 14.9.2: (a) the researchers identify the individual who conducted the interviews, (b) the researchers state when and where the interviews were conducted, and (c) the researchers indicate the basis for developing the interview guide.

Example 14.9.2

The primary author interviewed families three times in their homes for 3–6 months after the hospitalization of their child. The home was chosen as the most convenient and relaxed setting for parents of young children. The interview guide was modified for this study from an interview guide used by Chesla (1988) in her study of families coping with chronic illness in children. Parents were asked to describe how they evaluated symptoms [of asthma], assessed severity, managed compromised breathing in young children, took the step of seeking emergency care, and responded during hospitalization. [Seventeen] key interview questions are presented in Table 3.[11]

Providing details on data collection is also desirable when reporting on observational studies. Consider answering questions such as these when writing the description: Was the observer a participant or nonparticipant? When were the observations made? How often were they made? How were the data recorded? For what types of behaviors did the researcher initially look? What types of changes took place in the data collection method as the collection of data proceeded?

---

[10] Yeh et al. (2003, p. 486).
[11] Koenig & Chesla (2004, pp. 59–60).

➤ Guideline 14.10   Describe steps taken to ensure the trustworthiness of the data.

Qualitative researchers use a variety of methods to ensure that their data are trustworthy. These should be described in enough detail to reassure readers that the data are not merely the reflection of one researcher's personal opinions. For instance, when "member checks" are used, describe how the activity was conducted and by whom, as illustrated in Example 14.10.1.

Example 14.10.1

Before proceeding with the analysis of the focus group data, the major themes identified by the researchers as well as the examples selected to support the themes were presented in writing to a sample of 10 of the 20 participants. Although all 20 were invited to participate in this phase of the research, only 10 were available at the appointed time for this activity. The first stage of the member check was to have the 10 participants highlight with a marker those themes and examples that they deemed most important. They were also asked to cross out any that seemed to be off track or unrepresentative of their understandings of the members' meanings in the focus groups. The second stage was to hold two small-group meetings with five participants each to discuss the material they highlighted and crossed out. This activity was conducted by....

Likewise, if "triangulation of data sources" was used to ensure trustworthiness, describe what each source was (e.g., parents, children, and teachers) and specifically how the data were collected from each source. Also, if "triangulation of methods of data collection" was used (e.g., interviews as well as observations), describe each clearly.

As a general rule, the methods used to ensure trustworthiness, including others not mentioned here, should not be simply mentioned in passing in a research report. Instead, they should be described in some detail.

➤ Guideline 14.11   If two or more researchers participated in analyzing the data, describe how they arrived at a consensus.

In qualitative research, two or more individuals often participate in the analysis of the data. When this is done, readers will be interested in knowing about the extent to which these individuals were in agreement. Questions that might be addressed in light of this guideline are: Did the researchers analyze the data independently and then confer, or did they analyze it together from the beginning? If there were disagreements on some aspects of the interpretation, how were they resolved? How confident does each researcher feel in the final interpretations presented in the report?

➤ **Guideline 14.12   In the Results section of a qualitative report, provide quantitative results on quantitative matters.**

Conducting qualitative research does not preclude the use of statistics in reports on the research because some matters naturally lend themselves to quantification. Note that the term "many" in Example 14.12.1 is a quantitative term because it clearly implies that some number of students had their heads down. Yet, the term "many" is unnecessarily vague if the researcher knows how many students or what percentage of students did this. The improved version is consistent with this guideline.

Example 14.12.1

Many of the students were observed to have their heads down on their desks during the mathematics lesson.

Improved Version of Example 14.12.1

About 25% of the students were observed to have their heads down on their desks during the mathematics lesson.

In short, just because the main analysis in a qualitative research project is nonquantitative does not rule out the use of statistics when they are appropriate.

➤ **Guideline 14.13   Consider using the major themes as subheadings in the Results section.**

Often, the results of qualitative research are described in terms of major and minor themes. If the Results section of a report on qualitative research is long, consider using the names of the major themes as subheadings. This will help readers follow the organization of the results. In a report on women who had Hepatitis C, the authors of Example 14.13.1 used the themes shown as subheadings.

Example 14.13.1

*Major themes used as subheadings (**in bold**) in the Results section*:
Seeking a diagnosis
   Our respondents' encounter with Hepatitis C began in 1977, some 12 years before the virus was....
Constructing alternative explanations
   When mainstream medicine failed to identify a reason for their ill health, individual women constructed various kinds of explanations....
Labile emotional reactions to the diagnosis
   Initially, participants were relieved, as the following excerpts illustrate....

Concern about emerging dysfunction

Cognitive dysfunction in terms of failures of concentration, memory loss, difficulty in comprehending....

Progressive erosion of existing and expected roles

Role erosion emerged from the impact on everyday activities of the physical limitations that the women....

Negative impact on familial and other close relationships

The women's descriptions of the impact of their condition on relationships fell into four categories....

[Note: The writers used four subheadings for minor themes under **Negative impact on familial and other close relationships**. They are: **Social life with and within the family**, **Effect on partners**, **Effect on children**, and **Effect on relatives and friends**.][12]

➢ Guideline 14.14   If quotations are reported, consider stating the basis for their selection.

In qualitative research, large amounts of narrative material (the raw data) are often collected. Readers will be interested in learning the basis for the selection of the limited number of quotations presented in the Results section of a research report. Note that there may be different reasons for the selection of various quotations. Some might be selected because they are the most articulate expressions of a recurring theme. Others might be selected because they are the most emotional. The most common basis for selecting quotations is that they are *representative* of what a number of participants stated, which is illustrated in Example 14.14.1, in which the researchers indicate that the quotations illustrate a theme that was noted 21 times.

Example 14.14.1

The participants reported that they needed an external boost or push to get them to come to exercise and to keep them coming. They needed to be accountable to someone so they would not slack off or "cheat." This external boost was noted 21 times.

> "We need supervision! We need the instructor to help us keep it up or else we do not do it. At least once a week we need that external boost. It is not easy to do the exercise on your own!"

> "Most of us live alone so it is better to come and exercise in a group. I do not do too well at home as I cheat a little. When I am in the class I got to keep up. You do not want to cheat with the instructor."[13]

---

[12] Dunne & Quayle (2001, pp. 682–689).
[13] Resnick, Vogel, & Luisi (2006, p. 23).

> ➤ **Guideline 14.15   Consider discussing alternative interpretations of the data and why they were rejected.**

If there are obvious alternative interpretations, explicitly discuss the reasons for rejecting them in the Results section. For instance, a researcher might use quotations or talk about trends in the data that run counter to the alternatives, which would help explain why one interpretation was selected over another.

Concluding Comments

Writing effective reports of both qualitative and quantitative research is an art that can be mastered only with careful modeling of the writing of skilled professionals and practice. To move beyond this book and become a master of empirical research writing, the most important thing you can do is read numerous examples of the research written by others—with attention to detail, style, and mechanics. Skimming articles or, worse yet, reading only the abstracts is not sufficient. Instead, you should read research reports in their entirety while evaluating them by asking questions such as the following: What makes a report effective or ineffective? At what points did you get lost while reading a report? What else could the researcher have done to assist you in following his or her line of reasoning? In short, by becoming a critical consumer of research written by others, you will become a skilled writer of empirical research reports.

Exercise for Chapter 14

PART A

1. According to this chapter, is it more appropriate to put the term *qualitative* in a subtitle *or* to put it in the main title? Explain.

2. According to this chapter, when is it especially important to discuss the choice of qualitative methods over quantitative methods in a research report?

3. Because qualitative research often involves direct interactions between researchers and participants, what should researchers consider describing?

4. How is a *purposive sample* defined in this chapter?

5. When should researchers refer to their sample as a "sample of convenience"?

6. According to this chapter, is it ever appropriate to use statistics to present demographic information in a qualitative study?

7. According to this chapter, methods used to ensure trustworthiness should not be simply mentioned in passing in a research report. Instead, what should be done?

8. If two or more researchers participated in analyzing the data, what should be described in the research report?

9. Is it ever desirable to report quantities in the Results section of a report on qualitative research?

10. According to this chapter, what is the most common basis for selecting quotations from participants to include in a report on qualitative research?

11. Should alternative interpretations of the data be discussed in a qualitative research report?

PART B: Locate a report on qualitative research that you think illustrates many of the guidelines in this chapter. Bring it to class for discussion.

Notes

Chapter 15
Preparing Reference Lists[1]

The reference list is usually the last element in a research report.[2] Researchers will cite mainly journal articles in their research reports because journal articles are the major source of primary (i.e., original) reports of the research of others. Thus, this chapter emphasizes the preparation of a reference list that refers to journal articles. For details on referencing other types of sources, consult a style manual (see Guideline 15.2).

> ➤ **Guideline 15.1   "References" is a main heading that follows the main heading "Discussion."**

Example 15.1.1 shows the placement of the Reference list relative to the other parts of a research report discussed up to this point in this book (see the arrow in the Example).

> **Example 15.1.1**
>
> Title in Upper- and Lowercase Letters
> **Abstract** (a main heading; centered in bold)
> A literature review that introduces the research problem (with no heading)
> **Method** (a main heading; centered in bold)
> **Participants** (a subheading; flush left in bold)
> **Measures** (a subheading; flush left in bold)
> **Procedure** (optional; a subheading; flush left in bold)
> **Analysis** (optional; a subheading; flush left in bold)
> **Results** (a main heading; centered in bold)
> **Discussion** (a main heading; centered in bold)
> ⇨**References** (a main heading; centered in bold)

> ➤ **Guideline 15.2   Select a style manual and carefully follow its directions for preparing a reference list.**

A style manual specifies mechanical features such as spacing, margins, and levels of heading, as well as the preparation of reference lists for manuscripts written for a particular audience. For instance, the *Publication Manual of the American Psychological Association* prescribes mechanics for the preparation of manuscripts for publication in the journals published by the Association. Because of its comprehensive nature, it is also the style manual

---

[1] Portions of this chapter were adopted with permission from Pan (2008).
[2] If there are appendices to a research report, these should be included after the reference list.

for many journals in other fields such as education, sociology, nursing, and physical education.

Example 15.2.1 shows a reference list entry for a journal article formatted in American Psychological Association (APA) style. Notice that many of the details of the style cannot be derived from intuition. For instance, the first and middle names of authors are not spelled out and, the "&" sign, not the word *and*, is used when there are multiple authors. Also, APA style does not use the abbreviation "pp." before the page numbers (e.g., 280–288 in Example 15.2.1 is *not* preceded with "pp.").

Example 15.2.1

Allen, E. S., Rhoades, G. K., Stanley, S. M., & Markman, H. J. (2010). Hitting home: Relationships between recent deployment, posttraumatic stress symptoms, and marital functioning for Army couples. *Journal of Family Psychology, 24,* 280–288.

Notice the use of a *hanging indent* (i.e., the first line is not indented but the subsequent lines in the reference are indented) in Example 15.2.1. The hanging indent makes the authors' names stand out in a reference list (examine the reference list after this chapter).[3]

> ➢ **Guideline 15.3 A journal title is treated like a book title—either underline or italicize it.**

Traditional academic libraries usually collect all the issues of a journal for a year and have them case bound (i.e., put into a hardback cover). This results in a "book" for each year of the journal. As with any other book, underline or italicize the titles of journals.

> ➢ **Guideline 15.4 While volume numbers are important in identifying a journal article, issue numbers are not.**

Certain conventions in numbering journals are almost always followed. For instance, each issue of a journal has an issue number, almost always with "1" for the first issue of a year, "2" for the second issue of a year, and so on. All issues within a year have a volume number. Thus, the volume number *26* (italicized) in Example 15.4.1 indicates that the reference is in the volume published in the 26th year of the journal's existence.

---

[3] In Microsoft Word, a hanging indent can be easily created by clicking on "Format," then "Paragraph," which will default to the "Indents and Spacing" dialog box. To reveal the word "Hanging," click on the down arrow under the word "Special." Then click on the word "Hanging" to create a hanging indent.

Example 15.4.1

Goldstein, S. E., & Tisak, M. S. (2010). Early adolescents' conceptions of parental and friend authority over relational aggression. *Journal of Early Adolescence, 26,* 344–364.

Within each volume, page numbers are consecutive. Thus, the first issue of a journal for a year begins with page 1. If that issue ends on page 222, then the next issue for the same year begins with page 223. Thus, when all issues for a year (i.e., the volume) are case bound by a library, each page in a volume has a unique number. Hence, issue numbers can be omitted in reference lists without a loss of information essential to locating an article.

➤ **Guideline 15.5   Double-check punctuation in accordance with the style manual.**

A style manual specifies the punctuation to be used in a reference list. For instance, if a style manual shows a period at the close of the parentheses containing the year of publication, be careful not to substitute a comma.

➤ **Guideline 15.6   Double-check capitalization in accordance with the style manual.**

In APA style, for instance, only the first letter of the first word in the main title and in the subtitle of the journal article begins with capital letters. Capping the letters of all major words in the title in a reference list is not APA style.[4]

➤ **Guideline 15.7   A reference list should contain entries only for those that have been cited in the research report.**

Do not treat the reference list as a suggested reading list. Include only references for literature that was cited in the body of the research report.

➤ **Guideline 15.8   Cross-check reference citations in the body of the report with those in the reference list.**

Examine each citation in the body of the research report and check to see that (a) it is included in the reference list, (b) names are spelled correctly in both places, and (c) years of publication are the same.

---

[4] Also, proper names should be capitalized. This guideline applies only to the reference list. The first letters of all major words in the title of a research report (i.e., the title that appears at the beginning of the report) should be capitalized.

Concluding Comments

Preparing a reference list should be done with great care. Inaccurate or improperly formatted references can cost points when term-project reports are graded. In addition, carelessness could call into question the care with which other parts of a report were prepared.

Exercise for Chapter 15

1. What is missing from the following reference?

   Jones, B. F., & Smith, A. D. (2010). The relationship between job satisfaction and income level. *Journal of Labor*, 14–20.

2. What is missing from the following reference?

   Jones, B. F., Smith, A. D. (2011). The relationship between job satisfaction and income level. *Journal of Labor*, 35, 14–20.

3. Are italics used appropriately in the following reference? Explain.

   Jones, B. F., & Smith, A. D. (2009). *The relationship between job satisfaction and income level.* Journal of Labor, 35, 14–20.

4. What should be deleted from the following reference?

   Jones, B. F., & Smith, A. D. (2010). The relationship between job satisfaction and income level. *Journal of Labor, 35,* pp. 14–20.

5. What should be changed in the following reference?

   Jones, Bernard F., & Smith, Amy D. (2011). The relationship between job satisfaction and income level. *Journal of Labor, 35,* 14–20.

6. What is wrong with the punctuation in the following reference?

   Jones, B. F., & Smith, A. D. (2009), The relationship between job satisfaction and income level. *Journal of Labor, 35,* 14–20.

7. What is wrong with the capitalization in the following reference?

   Jones, B. F., & Smith, A. D. (2010). The Relationship Between Job Satisfaction and Income Level. *Journal of Labor, 35,* 14–20.

References

Alfaro, E. C., Umaña-Taylor, A. J., & Bámaca, M. Y. (2006). The influence of academic support on Latino adolescents' academic motivation. *Family Relations, 55,* 279–291.

Allen, E. S., Rhoades, G. K., Stanley, S. M., & Markman, H. J. (2010). Hitting home: Relationships between recent deployment, posttraumatic stress symptoms, and marital functioning for Army couples. *Journal of Family Psychology, 24,* 280–288.

Altman, J. C. (2003). A qualitative examination of client participation in agency-initiated services. *Families in Society: The Journal of Contemporary Human Service, 84,* 471–479.

Alvarenga, M. D., Scagliusi, F. B., & Philippi, S. T. (2010). Development and validity of the disordered eating attitude scale (DEAS). *Perceptual and Motor Skills, 110,* 379–395.

Beck, C. T., & Watson, S. (2010). Subsequent childbirth after a previous traumatic birth. *Nursing Research, 59,* 241–249.

Behnke, A. O., Piercy, K. W., & Diversi, M. (2004). Educational and occupational aspirations of Latino youth and their parents. *Hispanic Journal of Behavioral Sciences, 26,* 16–35.

Brechting, E. H., Brown, T. L., Salsman, J. M., Sauer, S. E., Holeman, V. T., & Carlson, C. R. (2010). The role of religious beliefs and behaviors in predicting underage alcohol use. *Journal of Child & Adolescent Substance Abuse, 19,* 324–334.

Bushman, B. B., & Peacock, G. G. (2010). Does teaching problem-solving skills matter? An evaluation of problem-solving skills training for the treatment of social and behavioral problems in children. *Child & Family Behavior Therapy, 32,* 103–124.

Caetano, R., Ramisetty-Mikler, S., & McGrath, C. (2004). Acculturation, drinking, and intimate partner violence among Hispanic couples in the United States: A longitudinal study. *Hispanic Journal of Behavioral Science, 26,* 60–78.

Carbonaro, W., & Covay, E. (2010). School sector and student achievement in the era of standards based reforms. *Sociology of Education, 83,* 160–182.

Chen, K.-M., Fan, J.-T., Wang, H.-H., Wu, S.-J., Li, C.-H., & Lin, H.-S. (2010). Silver yoga exercises improved physical fitness of transitional frail elders. *Nursing Research, 59,* 364–370.

Collins, N., Hymon-Parker, S., Mitstifer, D. I., & Nelson Goff, B. S. (2010). Perceptions of the value of undergraduate research: A pilot qualitative study of human sciences graduates. *Family & Consumer Sciences Research Journal, 38,* 303–316.

Constantine, M. G., Alleyne, V. L., Caldwell, L. D., McRae, M. B., & Suzuki, L. A. (2006). Coping responses of Asian, Black, and Latino/Latina New York City residents following the September 11, 2001 terrorist attacks against the United States. *Cultural Diversity and Ethnic Minority Psychology, 11,* 293–308.

Corning, A. F., Krumm, A. J., & Smitham, L. A. (2006). Differential social comparison processes in women with and without eating disorder symptoms. *Journal of Counseling Psychology, 53,* 338–349.

Covay, E., & Carbonaro, W. (2010). After the bell: Participation in extracurricular activities, classroom behavior, and academic achievement. *Sociology of Education, 83,* 20–45.

Cukrowicz, K. C., Otamendi, A., Pinto, J. V., Bernert, R. A., Krakow, B., & Joiner, T. E. (2006). The impact of insomnia and sleep disturbances on depression and suicidality. *Dreaming, 16,* 1–10.

Daurat, A., Huet, N., & Tiberge, M. (2010). Metamemory beliefs and episodic memory in obstructive sleep apnea syndrome. *Psychological Reports, 107,* 289–302.

Diemer, M. A., Kauffman, A., Koenig, N., Trahan, E., & Hsieh, C.-A. (2006). Challenging racism, sexism, and social injustice: Support for urban adolescents' critical consciousness development. *Cultural Diversity and Ethnic Minority Psychology, 12,* 444–460.

Distefano, G., & Hohman, M. (2010). Selecting strategic counseling interventions for DUI clients. *Journal of Social Work Practice in the Addictions, 10,* 180–196.

Dohnt, H., & Tiggemann, M. (2006). The contribution of peer and media influences to the development of body satisfaction and self-esteem in young girls: A prospective study. *Developmental Psychology, 42,* 929–936.

Dunne, E. A., & Quayle, E. (2001). The impact of iatrogenically acquired Hepatitis C infection on the well-being and relationships of a group of Irish women. *Journal of Health Psychology, 6,* 679–692.

Fleming, C. B., White, H. R., & Catalano, R. F. (2010). Romantic relationships and substance use in early adulthood: An examination of the influences of relationship type, partner substance use, and relationship quality. *Journal of Health and Social Behavior, 51,* 153–167.

Foster, L. S., & Keele, R. (2006). Implementing an over-the-counter medication administration policy in an elementary school. *Journal of School Nursing, 22,* 108–113.

Fredricks, J. A., Alfeld-Liro, C., Hruda, L. Z., Eccles, J. S., Patrick, H., & Ryan, A. M. (2002). A qualitative exploration of adolescents' commitment to athletics and the arts. *Journal of Adolescent Research, 17,* 68–97.

Frone, M. R. (2006). Prevalence and distribution of illicit drug use in the workforce and in the workplace: Findings and implications from a U.S. national survey. *Journal of Applied Psychology, 91,* 856–869.

Greder, K., Sano, Y., Cook, C. C., Garasky, S., Ortiz, L., & Ontai, L. (2009). Exploring relationships between transnationalism and housing and health risks of rural Latino immigrant families. *Family & Consumer Sciences Research Journal, 38,* 186–207.

Guilamo-Ramos, V., Dittus, P., Jaccard, J., Goldberg, V., Casillas, E., & Bouris, A. (2006). The content and process of mother–adolescent communication about sex in Latino families. *Social Work Research, 30,* 169–181.

Hammond, W. P., & Mattis, J. S. (2005). Being a man about it: Manhood meaning among African American men. *Psychology of Men and Masculinity, 6,* 114–126.

Harrison, R., MacFarlane, A., Murray, E., & Wallace, P. (2006). Patients' perceptions of joint teleconsultations: A qualitative evaluation. *Health Expectations: An International Journal of Public Participation in Health Care & Health Policy, 9,* 81–90.

Higgins, C. A., Duxbury, L. E., & Lyons, S. T. (2010). Coping with overload and stress: Men and women in dual-earner families. *Journal of Marriage and Family, 72,* 847–859.

Hutchinson, D. M., Rapee, R. M., & Taylor, A. (2010). Body dissatisfaction and eating disturbances in early adolescence: A structural modeling investigation examining negative affect and peer factors. *Journal of Early Adolescence, 30,* 489–517.

Ilies, R., & Judge, T. A. (2005). Goal regulation across time: The effects of feedback and affect. *Journal of Applied Psychology, 90,* 453–467.

Iwamoto, D. K., Liao, L., & Liu, W. M. (2010). Masculine norms, avoidant coping, Asian values, and depression among Asian American men. *Psychology of Men & Masculinity, 11,* 15–24.

Jacob, C. M. A., & Veach, P. M. (2005). Intrapersonal and familial effects of child sexual abuse on female partners of male survivors. *Journal of Counseling Psychology, 52,* 284–297.

Jones, C. D., Reutzel, D. R., & Fargo, J. D. (2010). Comparing two methods of writing instruction: Effects on kindergarten students' reading skills. *The Journal of Educational Research, 103,* 327–341.

Knight, G. P., Gonzales, N. A., Saenz, D. S., Bonds, D. D., Germán, M., Deardorff, J., Roosav, M. W., & Updegraff, K. A. (2010). The Mexican American cultural values scale for adolescents and adults. *Journal of Early Adolescence, 30,* 444–481.

Koenig, K., & Chesla, C. A. (2004). Asthma management among low-income Latino and African American families of infants and young children. *Family Relations, 53,* 58–67.

Koren, I., Mian, O., & Rukholm, E. (2010). Integration of nurse practitioners into Ontario's primary health care system: Variations across practice settings. *Canadian Journal of Nursing Research, 42,* 48–69.

Lightsey, O. W., & Hulsey, C. D. (2002). Impulsivity, coping, stress, and problem gambling among university students. *Journal of Counseling Psychology, 49,* 202–211.

Lopez-Williams, A., Stoep, A. V., Kuo, E., & Stewart, D. G. (2006). Predictors of mental health service enrollment among juvenile offenders. *Youth Violence and Juvenile Justice, 4,* 266–280.

Mancha, B. E., Rojas-Neese, V. C., & Latimer, W. W. (2010). Alcohol use problem severity and problem behavior engagement among school-based youths in Minnesota. *Journal of Child & Adolescent Substance Abuse, 19*, 210–222.

Mancini, A. D., & Bonanno, G. A. (2006). Marital closeness, functional disability, and adjustment in late life. *Psychology and Aging, 21*, 600–610.

Mann, E. A., & Reynolds, A. J. (2006). Early intervention and juvenile delinquency prevention: Evidence from the Chicago Longitudinal Study. *Social Work Research, 30*, 153–167.

Marley, S. C., Levin, J. R., & Glenberg, A. M. (2010). What cognitive benefits does an activity-based reading strategy afford young Native American readers? *The Journal of Experimental Education, 78*, 395–417.

Mathews, T. L., Fawcett, S. B., & Sheldon, J. B. (2009). Effects of a peer engagement program on socially withdrawn children with a history of maltreatment. *Child & Family Behavior Therapy, 31*, 270–291.

Mazurik-Charles, R., & Stefanou, C. (2010). Using paraprofessionals to teach social skills to children with autism spectrum disorders in the general education classroom. *Journal of Instructional Psychology, 37*, 161–169.

McCreary, D. R., & Sadava, S. W. (2001). Gender differences in relationships among perceived attractiveness, life satisfaction, and health in adults as a function of body mass index and perceived weight. *Psychology of Men and Masculinity, 2*, 108–116.

McMahon, B. T., West, S. L., Lewis, A. N., Armstrong, A. J., & Conway, J. P. (2004). Hate crimes and disability in America. *Rehabilitation Counseling Bulletin, 47*, 66–75.

McNamara, R. S., Swaim, R. C., & Rosén, L. A. (2010). Components of negative affect as moderators of the relationship between early drinking onset and binge-drinking behavior. *Journal of Child & Adolescent Substance Abuse, 19*, 108–121.

Melenhorst, A.-S., Rogers, W. A., & Bouwhuis, D. G. (2006). Older adults' motivated choice for technological innovation: Evidence for benefit-driven selectivity. *Psychology and Aging, 21*, 190–195.

Mishima, T., Horimoto, A., & Mori, T. (2010). Changes in the images of teaching, teachers, and children expressed by student teachers before and after student teaching. *Psychological Reports, 106*, 769–784.

Monserud, M. A. (2010). Role markers of adulthood and young adults' ties to grandparents. *Journal of Intergenerational Relationships, 8*, 38–53.

Okamoto, S. K., Po'a-Kekuawela, K., Chin, C. I. H., Nebre, L. R. H., & Helm, S. (2010). Exploring culturally specific drug resistance strategies of Hawaiian youth in rural communities. *Journal of Alcohol and Drug Education, 54*, 56–75.

Ornes, L. L., & Ransdell, L. B. (2010). A pilot study examining exercise self-efficacy as a mediator for walking behavior in college-age women. *Perceptual and Motor Skills, 110*, 1098–1104.

Owens, M. R., & Bergman, A. (2010). Alcohol use and antisocial behavior in late adolescence: Characteristics of a sample attending a GED program. *Journal of Child & Adolescent Substance Abuse, 19*, 78–98.

Pan, M. L. (2008). *Preparing literature reviews: Qualitative and quantitative approaches* (3rd ed.). Glendale, CA: Pyrczak Publishing.

Parish, T., Baghurst, T., & Turner, R. (2010). Becoming competitive amateur bodybuilders: Identification of contributors. *Psychology of Men & Masculinity, 11*, 152–159.

Planken, M. J. E., & Boer, H. (2010). Effects of a 10-minute peer education protocol to reduce binge drinking among adolescents during holidays. *Journal of Alcohol and Drug Education, 54*, 35–52.

Reeves, J. S., & Fogg, C. (2006). Perceptions of graduating nursing students regarding life experiences that promote culturally competent care. *Journal of Transcultural Nursing, 17*, 171–178.

Resnick, B., Vogel, A., & Luisi, D. (2006). Motivating minority older adults to exercise. *Cultural Diversity and Ethnic Minority Psychology, 12*, 17–29.

Robins, S. (2010). Ambiguous loss in a non-Western context: Families of the disappeared in post-conflict Nepal. *Family Relations, 59*, 253–268.

Rodham, K., Brewer, H., Mistral, W., & Stallard, P. (2006). Adolescents' perception of risk and challenge: A qualitative study. *Journal of Adolescence, 29*, 261–272.

Russell, B., Kraus, S. W., & Ceccherini, T. (2010). Student perceptions of aggressive behaviors and predictive patterns of perpetration and victimization: The role of age and sex. *Journal of School Violence, 9*, 251–270.

Scott, L. D., Hofmeister, N., Rogness, N., & Rogers, A. E. (2010). An interventional approach for patient and nurse safety: A fatigue countermeasures feasibility study. *Nursing Research, 59*, 250–258.

Simoni, J. M., Frick, P. A., & Huang, B. (2006). A longitudinal evaluation of a social support model of medication adherence among HIV-positive men and women on antiretroviral therapy. *Health Psychology, 25*, 74–81.

Sira, N., & Ballard, S. M. (2009). An ecological approach to examining body satisfaction in Caucasian and African American female college students. *Family & Consumer Sciences Research Journal, 38*, 208–226.

Smith, H., Varjas, K., Meyers, J., Marshall, M. L., Ruffner, C., & Graybill, E. C. (2010). Teachers' perceptions of teasing in schools. *Journal of School Violence, 9*, 2–22.

Steinhauser, M., & Hübner, R. (2006). Response-based strengthening in task shifting: Evidence from shift effects produced by errors. *Journal of Experimental Psychology: Human Perception and Performance, 32*, 517–534.

Sullivan, C. J. (2006). Early adolescent delinquency: Assessing the role of childhood problems, family environment, and peer pressure. *Youth Violence and Juvenile Justice, 4*, 291–313.

Tarasenko, M. A., Miltenberger, R. G., Brower-Breitwieser, C., & Bosch, A. (2010). Evaluation of peer training for teaching abduction prevention skills. *Child & Family Behavior Therapy, 32*, 219–230.

Theokas, C., Almerigi, J. B., Lerner, R. M., Dowling, E. M., Benson, P. L., Scales, P. C., & von Eye, A. (2005). Conceptualizing and modeling individual and ecological asset components of thriving in early adolescence. *Journal of Early Adolescence, 25*, 113–143.

Thiede, H., Valleroy, L. A., MacKellar, D. A., Celentano, D. D., Ford, W. L., Hagan, H., Koblin, B. A., LaLota, M., McFarland, W., Shehan, D. A., & Torian, L. V. (2003). Regional patterns and correlates of substance use among young men who have sex with men in seven US urban areas. *American Journal of Public Health, 93*, 1915–1921.

Thomson, N. R., & Zand, D. H. (2010). Mentees' perceptions of their interpersonal relationships: The role of the mentor-youth bond. *Youth & Society, 41*, 434–445.

Vairo, E. (2010). Social worker attitudes toward court-mandated substance-abusing clients. *Journal of Social Work Practice in the Addictions, 10*, 81–98.

Wang, C.-Y. (2010). Hand dominance and grip strength of older Asian adults. *Perceptual and Motor Skills, 110*, 897–900.

Watkins, A. M., & Melde, C. (2010). Latino and Asian students' perceptions of the quality of their educators: The role of generational status and language proficiency. *Youth & Society, 42*, 3–32.

Weintraub, A. P. C., & Killian, T. S. (2009). Perceptions of the impact of intergenerational programming on the physical well-being of participants in adult day services. *Journal of Intergenerational Relationships, 7*, 355–370.

Whiting, J. B., & Lee, R. E., III. (2003). Voices from the system: A qualitative study of foster children's stories. *Family Relations, 52*, 288–295.

Williams, R. J., & Connolly, D. (2006). Does learning about the mathematics of gambling change gambling behavior? *Psychology of Addictive Behaviors, 20*, 62–68.

Wood, J. (2006). Effect of anxiety reduction on children's school performance and social adjustment. *Developmental Psychology, 42*, 345–349.

Yeh, C. J., Arora, A. K., Inose, M., Okubo, Y., Li, R. H., & Greene, P. (2003). The cultural adjustment and mental health of Japanese immigrant youth. *Adolescence, 38*, 481–500.

Yildirim, N. Ü., Erbahçecí, F., Ergun, N., Pitetti, K. H., & Beets, M. W. (2010). The effect of physical fitness training on reaction time in youth with intellectual disabilities. *Perceptual and Motor Skills, 111*, 178–186.

Yip, K., Ngan, M., & Lam, I. (2003). A qualitative study of parental influence on and response to adolescents' self-cutting in Hong Kong. *Families in Society: The Journal of Contemporary Human Services, 84*, 405–416.

Zajacova, A., & Burgard, S. A. (2010). Body weight and health from early to mid-adulthood: A longitudinal analysis. *Journal of Health and Social Behavior, 51*, 92–107.

Notes

Appendix A
Checklist of Guidelines

Instructors may wish to refer to the following checklist numbers when commenting on students' papers (e.g., "See Guideline 5.2"). Students can use this checklist to review important points as they prepare their research reports and proposals.

Chapter 1 Structuring a Research Report

___ 1.1 A research report typically has a brief title.

___ 1.2 An abstract usually follows the title.

___ 1.3 The body of a typical research report begins with a literature review, which serves as the introduction to the research project.

___ 1.4 The Method section describes the participants, the measures, and other details on how the research was conducted.

___ 1.5 The Results section presents the findings.

___ 1.6 The Discussion section presents the researcher's interpretations.

___ 1.7 The reference list should contain references only to literature cited in the report.

___ 1.8 In long reports, use additional second-level and third-level headings.

Chapter 2 Writing Simple Research Hypotheses

___ 2.1 A simple research hypothesis should name two variables and indicate the type of relationship expected between them.

___ 2.2 When there is an independent variable, name a specific dependent variable.

___ 2.3 Consider naming population(s) in the hypothesis.

___ 2.4 A simple hypothesis should usually be expressed in a single sentence.

___ 2.5 Even a simple hypothesis should be as specific as possible within a single sentence.

___ 2.6 If a comparison is to be made, the elements to be compared should be stated.

___ 2.7 Because most hypotheses deal with the behavior of groups, plural forms should usually be used.

___ 2.8 Avoid sex-role stereotypes in the statement of a hypothesis.

___ 2.9 A hypothesis should be free of terms and phrases that do not add to its meaning.

____ 2.10 A hypothesis should indicate what will actually be studied—not the possible implications of a study or value judgments of the author.

____ 2.11 A hypothesis usually should name variables in the order in which they occur or will be measured.

____ 2.12 Avoid using the words *significant* or *significance* in a hypothesis.

____ 2.13 Avoid using the word *prove* in a hypothesis.

____ 2.14 Avoid using two different terms to refer to the same variable in a hypothesis.

____ 2.15 Avoid making precise statistical predictions in a hypothesis.

Chapter 3 A Closer Look at Hypotheses

____ 3.1 A single sentence may contain more than one hypothesis.

____ 3.2 When a number of related hypotheses are to be stated, consider presenting them in a numbered or lettered list.

____ 3.3 The hypothesis or hypotheses should be stated before the Method section.

____ 3.4 While some researchers use alternative terms, the term *hypothesis* is preferred.

____ 3.5 In a research report, a hypothesis should flow from the narrative that immediately precedes it.

____ 3.6 Both directional and nondirectional hypotheses are acceptable.

____ 3.7 When a researcher has a research hypothesis, it should be stated; the null hypothesis need not always be stated.

Chapter 4 Writing Research Objectives and Questions

____ 4.1 When no relationship will be examined, consider stating a research objective.

____ 4.2 When no relationship will be examined, consider posing a research question.

____ 4.3 Stating a research objective or posing a research question are equally acceptable.

____ 4.4 Avoid writing a research question that implies that the answer will be a simple "yes" or "no."

____ 4.5 When previous research is contradictory, consider using a research objective or a research question instead of a hypothesis.

____ 4.6 When a new topic is to be examined, consider using a research objective or a research question instead of a hypothesis.

____ 4.7 For *qualitative* research, consider writing a research objective or question instead of a hypothesis.

____ 4.8 A research objective or question should be as specific as possible, yet be comprehensible.

____ 4.9 When stating related objectives or questions, consider presenting them in a numbered or lettered list.

____ 4.10 A research objective or question should flow from the literature review that immediately precedes it.

Chapter 5 Writing Titles

____ 5.1 If only a small number of variables is studied, the title should name the variables.

____ 5.2 A title should not be a complete sentence.

____ 5.3 If many variables are studied, only the *types* of variables should be named.

____ 5.4 The title of a journal article should be concise; the title of a thesis or dissertation may be longer.

____ 5.5 A title should indicate what was studied—not the findings of the study.

____ 5.6 Consider mentioning the population(s) in a title.

____ 5.7 Consider the use of subtitles to indicate the methods of study.

____ 5.8 If a study is strongly tied to a particular model or theory, consider mentioning it in the title.

____ 5.9 Omit the names of specific measures unless they are the focus of the research.

____ 5.10 A title may be in the form of a question, but this form should be used sparingly and with caution.

____ 5.11 In titles, use the words *effect* and *influence* with caution.

____ 5.12 A title should be consistent with the research hypothesis, objective, purpose, or question.

____ 5.13 Consider mentioning unique features of a study in its title.

____ 5.14 Avoid using "clever" titles.

____ 5.15 Learn the conventions for capitalization in titles.

Chapter 6 Writing Introductions and Literature Reviews

____ 6.1 In theses and dissertations, the first chapter is usually an introduction.

____ 6.2 In theses and dissertations, the second chapter presents a comprehensive literature review.

____ 6.3 In most research reports, literature reviews serve as the introduction to the reports.

____ 6.4 In most research reports, literature reviews are selective.

____ 6.5 A literature review should be an essay—not a list of annotations.

____ 6.6 A literature review should lead logically to research hypotheses, objectives, or questions.

____ 6.7 Research hypotheses, objectives, or questions should usually be stated at the end of the literature review.

____ 6.8 Research reports with similar findings or methodologies should usually be cited together.

___ 6.9 The importance of a topic should be explicitly stated.

___ 6.10 Consider pointing out the number or percentage of individuals who are affected by the problem.

___ 6.11 Discuss theories that have relevance to the current research.

___ 6.12 Consider commenting on the relevance and importance of the research being cited.

___ 6.13 Point out trends in the literature.

___ 6.14 Point out gaps in the literature.

___ 6.15 Be prepared to justify statements regarding gaps in the literature.

___ 6.16 Point out how the current study differs from previous studies.

___ 6.17 Use direct quotations sparingly.

___ 6.18 Report sparingly on the details of the literature being cited.

___ 6.19 Consider using literature to provide the historical context for the present study.

___ 6.20 Consider citing prior literature reviews.

___ 6.21 When using the "author-date method" for citing references, decide whether to emphasize authorship or content.

___ 6.22 Avoid referring to the credentials and affiliations of the researchers.

___ 6.23 Terminology in a literature review should reflect the tentative nature of empirical data.

___ 6.24 Avoid using long strings of reference citations for a single finding or theory.

___ 6.25 Use of the first person is acceptable if used sparingly.

___ 6.26 In long literature reviews, start with a paragraph that describes their organization and use subheadings.

___ 6.27 Consider ending long and complex literature reviews with a brief summary.

Chapter 7 Writing Definitions

___ 7.1 All variables in a research hypothesis, objective, or question should be defined.

___ 7.2 The defining attributes of a population (also called *control variables*) should be defined.

___ 7.3 Key concepts in theories on which the research is based should be defined.

___ 7.4 A conceptual definition should be sufficiently specific to differentiate it from related concepts.

___ 7.5 Consider quoting published conceptual definitions.

___ 7.6 Consider providing examples to amplify conceptual definitions.

___ 7.7 Operational definitions usually should be provided in the Method section of a report.

___ 7.8 Consider providing operational definitions for each conceptual definition.

____ 7.9   If a published measure was used, the variable measured by it may be operationally defined by citing reference(s).

____ 7.10 If an unpublished measure was used, consider reproducing sample questions or the entire measure.

____ 7.11 Operational definitions should be specific enough so that another researcher can replicate the study.

____ 7.12 Even a highly operational definition may not be a useful definition.

Chapter 8 Writing Assumptions, Limitations, and Delimitations

____ 8.1   When stating an assumption, consider providing the reason(s) why it was necessary to make the assumption.

____ 8.2   If there is a reason for believing that an assumption is true, state the reason.

____ 8.3   If an assumption is highly questionable, consider casting it as a limitation.

____ 8.4   Distinguish between limitations and delimitations.

____ 8.5   Discuss limitations and delimitations separately.

____ 8.6   Consider elaborating on the nature of a limitation.

____ 8.7   Consider speculating on the possible effects of a limitation on the results of a study.

____ 8.8   If a study has serious limitations, consider labeling it a pilot study.

____ 8.9   Consider pointing out strengths as well as limitations.

Chapter 9 Writing Method Sections

____ 9.1   First, describe the participants.

____ 9.2   Decide whether to use the term *participants* or *subjects* to refer to the individuals studied.

____ 9.3   Describe the informed consent procedures, if any.

____ 9.4   Consider describing steps taken to maintain confidentiality of the data.

____ 9.5   The participants should be described in enough detail for the reader to visualize them.

____ 9.6   Consider reporting demographics in tables.

____ 9.7   When a sample is very small, consider providing a description of individual participants.

____ 9.8   If only a sample was studied, the method of sampling should be described.

____ 9.9   Explicitly acknowledge weaknesses in sampling.

____ 9.10 Provide detailed information on nonparticipants when possible.

____ 9.11 Describe the measures after describing the participants.

____ 9.12 Describe the traits a measure was designed to measure, its format, and the possible range of score values.

___ 9.13 Summarize information on reliability and validity, when available.

___ 9.14 Provide references where more information on the measures can be found.

___ 9.15 Consider providing sample items or questions.

___ 9.16 Make unpublished measures available.

Chapter 10 Describing Experimental Methods

___ 10.1 Describe experimental methods under the subheading "Procedure" under the main heading of "Method."

___ 10.2 If there are two or more groups, explicitly state how the groups were formed.

___ 10.3 Distinguish between *random selection* and *random assignment*.

___ 10.4 For experiments with only one participant, describe the length of each condition.

___ 10.5 Describe the experimental treatment in detail.

___ 10.6 Describe physical controls over the administration of the experimental treatment.

___ 10.7 Describe the control condition.

___ 10.8 Describe steps taken to reduce the "expectancy effect."

___ 10.9 If there was attrition, describe the dropouts.

___ 10.10 If participants were debriefed, mention it.

Chapter 11 Writing Analysis and Results Sections

___ 11.1 "Analysis" is a subheading under the main heading of "Method."

___ 11.2 The Analysis subsection is used sparingly in reports on quantitative research.

___ 11.3 The Analysis subsection is usually included in reports on qualitative research.

___ 11.4 "Results" is a main heading that follows the main heading "Method."

___ 11.5 Organize the Results section around the research hypotheses, objectives, or questions.

___ 11.6 It is usually not necessary to show formulas or calculations in either the Analysis or Results sections.

___ 11.7 The scores of individual participants usually are not shown.

___ 11.8 Present descriptive statistics before inferential statistics.

___ 11.9 Organize large numbers of statistics in tables.

___ 11.10 Give each table a number and caption (i.e., a descriptive title).

___ 11.11 Refer to statistical tables by number within the text of the Results section.

___ 11.12 When describing the statistics presented in a table, point out only the highlights.

___ 11.13 Statistical figures (e.g., drawings such as bar graphs) should be used sparingly.

___ 11.14 Statistical symbols should be underlined or italicized.

___ 11.15 Use the proper case for each statistical symbol.

___ 11.16 Consider when to spell out numbers.

___ 11.17 Qualitative results should be organized and the organization made clear to the reader.

Chapter 12 Writing Discussion Sections

___ 12.1 "Discussion" is a main heading that follows the main heading "Results."

___ 12.2 Consider starting the Discussion with a summary.

___ 12.3 Early in the Discussion section, refer to the research hypotheses, objectives, or questions.

___ 12.4 Point out whether results of the current study are consistent with the literature described in the literature review.

___ 12.5 Consider interpreting the results and offering explanations for them in the Discussion section.

___ 12.6 Mention important strengths and limitations in the Discussion section.

___ 12.7 It is usually inappropriate to introduce new data or new references in the Discussion section.

___ 12.8 When possible, state specific implications in the Discussion section.

___ 12.9 Be specific when making recommendations for future research.

___ 12.10 Consider using subheadings within the Discussion section.

Chapter 13 Writing Abstracts

___ 13.1 Determine the maximum length permissible for an abstract.

___ 13.2 If space permits, consider beginning an abstract by describing the general problem area.

___ 13.3 If space is limited, consider beginning by summarizing the research hypotheses, objectives, or questions.

___ 13.4 Highlights of the methodology should be summarized.

___ 13.5 Highlights of the results should be included.

___ 13.6 Point out any unexpected results.

___ 13.7 If a study is strongly tied to a theory, name the theory in the abstract.

___ 13.8 Mention any unique aspects of a study.

___ 13.9 Mention if a line of inquiry is new.

___ 13.10 If implications and suggestions for future research are emphasized in the report, consider concluding the abstract by mentioning them.

___ 13.11 An abstract should usually be short; however, there are exceptions.

___ 13.12 Consider using subheadings in an abstract.

Chapter 14 A Closer Look at Writing Reports of Qualitative Research

___ 14.1   Consider using the term *qualitative* in the title of the report.

___ 14.2   Consider using the term *qualitative* in the abstract of the report.

___ 14.3   Consider discussing the choice of qualitative over quantitative methodology.

___ 14.4   Consider "revealing yourself" to the readers.

___ 14.5   Avoid calling a sample *purposive* if it is actually a sample of convenience.

___ 14.6   If a purposive sample was used, state the basis for selection of participants.

___ 14.7   Describe how participants were recruited.

___ 14.8   Provide demographic information.

___ 14.9   Provide specific information on data collection methods.

___ 14.10 Describe steps taken to ensure the trustworthiness of the data.

___ 14.11 If two or more researchers participated in analyzing the data, describe how they arrived at a consensus.

___ 14.12 In the Results section of a qualitative report, provide quantitative results on quantitative matters.

___ 14.13 Consider using the major themes as subheadings in the Results section.

___ 14.14 If quotations are reported, consider stating the basis for their selection.

___ 14.15 Consider discussing alternative interpretations of the data and why they were rejected.

Chapter 15 Preparing Reference Lists

___ 15.1   "References" is a main heading that follows the main heading "Discussion."

___ 15.2   Select a style manual and carefully follow its directions for preparing a reference list.

___ 15.3   A journal title is treated like a book title—either underline or italicize it.

___ 15.4   While volume numbers are important in identifying a journal article, issue numbers are not.

___ 15.5   Double-check punctuation in accordance with the style manual.

___ 15.6   Double-check capitalization in accordance with the style manual.

___ 15.7   A reference list should contain entries only for those that have been cited in the research report.

___ 15.8   Cross-check reference citations in the body of the report with those in the reference list.

Appendix B

Thinking Straight and Writing That Way[1]

Ann Robinson
University of Arkansas at Little Rock

Everyone who submits manuscripts to top-flight journals gets rejected by the reviewers more than once in his or her publishing career. Often the rejections seem, at best, inexplicable and, at worst, biased. Rejections sting.

In a cooler moment, the disappointed author looks over the rejected paper and tries to read the reviewers' comments more calmly. What do journal reviewers look for in a manuscript? What makes a submission publishable? How can you increase the likelihood that your work will be accepted? These are good questions for any would-be author—seasoned or new—to ask.

In general, sessions on publishing "how-to's" rarely get beyond the obligatory lecture on the importance of the idea. We are told that if the idea is good, we should carry out the research study and proceed to submit the work for publication. If the how-to-get-published session gets past the point of explaining that a good study is one that asks an important question, then we are told that a publishable study is one that is reasonably free of design flaws. It seems to me that these two points ought to be considered givens. Although it is not always easy to think of a good idea, translate it into a researchable question, and design a competent study, most of us already understand the importance of these things. What we want to know now is how to increase our chances of getting competent work published.

Over the last eight years, I have developed the following questions to use when reviewing research manuscripts. They are offered as one reviewer's "test" of the publishability of a manuscript and may be helpful as guides for the prospective author.

---

[1] Originally published in *Gifted Child Quarterly, 32*, 367–369 as "Thinking Straight and Writing That Way: Publishing in *Gifted Child Quarterly.*" Copyright 1988 by the National Association for Gifted Children. Reprinted with permission.

Reviewer Question 1: What's the point?

Early on in the first "quick read," I ask why I should be interested in this manuscript. Will this study fill a gap in the existing literature? Will this study reconcile apparently contradictory research results from studies already published? Is this study anchored to a real problem affecting the education and upbringing of children and youth? Is this study "newsworthy"? Does the author convince me in the first few paragraphs that this manuscript is going to present important information new to the field or be investigated from a fresh perspective?

The manuscripts that most effectively make their "point" often have brief introductions that state the essence of the issue in the first or last sentence of the first or second paragraph. As a reviewer, I look for that "essence of issue" sentence. It is a benchmark for clear thinking and writing.

Reviewer Question 2: Can I find the general research question?

Reviewer Question 2 is related to the first, but I am now looking for something a bit more technical. The general research question should be stated clearly, and it should serve as the lodestone for the specific questions generated for the study. Congruence is important here. If I were to take each of these specific questions and check them against the general question, I would easily see the connection. For example, in a study of the family systems of underachieving males, the general question is, "What are the interactional relationships within families of gifted students?" (Green, Fine, & Tollefson, 1988) Two specific questions derived from the general one are:

> (1) Is there a difference in the proportion of families of achieving and underachieving gifted students that are classified as functional and dysfunctional? (2) Do family members having achieving or underachieving gifted students differ in their satisfaction with their families? (p. 268)

The manuscripts that most effectively answered Reviewer Question 2 placed the general question at the end of the review of the literature. It will be stated as a question and prefaced with a lead-in like "the general purpose of this study" or "an important research question is." Then the specific questions for the study are enumerated and set apart in a list. The combination of text and visual cues makes it difficult for the reviewer to overlook the focus of the manuscript.

Reviewer Question 3: Can I get a "picture" of the participants of this study?

The appropriate level of description for the participants is difficult to judge. However, it is better to over- rather than underdescribe them. This is true whether the study is experimental or a naturalistic inquiry. Insufficient information about the participants in the study leaves the reviewer wondering if the conclusions are suspect. Would the results be the same if other participants had participated? Go beyond the breakdowns by age or grade, sex, and ethnicity. If the participants are students in a gifted program, describe the identification procedure. If the participants are school personnel, describe their professional positions, years in service, or other variables that might affect the results. As a reviewer, I always try to determine the extent to which a participant sample is volunteer and how seriously volunteerism might bias the results. If a study is conducted in one school building, district, or one teacher or parent advocate group, I look for descriptions of this context. How large is the school or organization? Is it rural, urban, or suburban? Who is responding to surveys? Fathers or mothers? Are families intact, single parent, or extended? What is the socioeconomic level?

For example, in a study of learning styles, Rica (1984) included the following information to give a thorough picture of the subjects.

> The study population included 425 students in grades four, five, and six from one city school and one suburban school district in western New York. Descriptive contrast groups represented participants who were identified as gifted and a contrast group taken from the remaining general school students available. Gifted students were identified by a multidimensional screening process with data sources indicated in Table 1. (p. 121)

This information is followed by a further explanation of the identification process and three brief tables that provide a tidy summary of student demographics and cognitive and academic characteristics. The combination of text and tables gives the reviewer a clear picture of the participants in the study.

The reviewer may ultimately ask the author to trim the text on participants, but overzealous descriptions serve two purposes. First, they demonstrate to the reviewer that the author is a careful worker. Second, they rein in generalizations, which appear in the Conclusions and Implications sections of the manuscript. An author may well be entitled to make statements about the population from which the sample of participants is drawn, but if the demographics of the group change, the conclusions may not be safely generalized.

The manuscripts that most effectively create a picture of their sample include the basics like age, grade, sex, and ethnicity succinctly, sometimes in tabled form. Case study researchers are less likely to use tables because of smaller samples, but they do identify the reasons why they believe a participant is representative of a large group. In studies of gifted children, the most effective manuscripts clearly state the selection procedure and identify specific instruments or checklists, if appropriate, under the Participants section of the paper.

Reviewer Question 4: Is this author killing flies with an elephant gun?

As a reviewer, I examine the manuscript for a comfortable fit among the research questions, the kinds of data that have been collected, and the tools of analysis. In the case of manuscripts that present quantitative data and statistical analyses, I apply Occam's razor. The simplest statistics are usually the best. A good research question can be insightfully investigated with relatively simple analyses provided the assumptions are not too badly violated. The purpose of statistics is to summarize and clarify, not to fog.

Of course, authors who seek to control confounded variables through the use of more sophisticated statistical treatments like the currently popular LISREL increase the likelihood that multiple causation is disentangled. We certainly gain from technological innovation; however, the key is to determine if the impetus for the study is a substantive research question or a fascination with the newest techniques.

The manuscripts that answer Reviewer Question 4 most effectively are those in which hypotheses do not sink under the weight of the analyses. As I read the Design and Analysis sections, am I able to keep my eye on the important variables? A good indicator is a sentence in the Design section that gives me the rationale for using quite sophisticated or new statistical and qualitative techniques. For example, a study of ethnic differences in a mathematics program for gifted students included the following explanation for the selection of a specialized kind of regression analysis (Robinson, Bradley, & Stanley, in review):

> Regression discontinuity is a quasi-experimental design that allows the experimenter to test for treatment effects without a randomized control group and the attendant withholding of services. This a priori design statistically controls for prior differences by using the identification variable along with

program participation (status) as independent variables in a multiple regression model. (p. 7)

Another indication that the study is being driven by its questions rather than its statistics is the author's effort to make connecting statements between a technique and its interpretation. To return to the previous regression example:

If the associated *t* test of the regression coefficient is significant, it is indicative of a program that impacts on its participants. (p. 7)

Reviewer Question 5: Would George Orwell approve?

Dogging the reviewer through both the "quick read" and the "close read" of the manuscript is the ease with which the author has answered the first four questions. If we look back at those questions, we see the common thread of clarity running through them. What is the point? Where is the question? Who is this study about? Does the analysis illuminate rather than obfuscate?

Reviewer Question 5 is the final test. Would George Orwell approve? In 1946, Orwell published "Politics and the English Language," one of the clearest statements on writing effectively ever to appear in print. The thesis of his essay was that "modern English, especially written English, is full of bad habits, which spread by imitation and which can be avoided if one is willing to take the necessary trouble . . . prose consists less and less of words chosen for the sake of their meaning, and more and more of phrases tacked together like sections of a prefabricated hen-house" (p. 159). Orwell was clearly unhappy with vague writing and professional jargon. He felt that poor writing was an indication of sloppy thinking, and he excused neither the social scientist nor the novelist from his strict dicta of good, vigorous writing. He had a particular dislike of using ready-made phrases like "lay the foundation," and he was equally appalled at the indiscriminate use of scientific terms to give the impression of objectivity to biased statements.

As a reviewer, I apply Orwell's tough rules to the test of every manuscript I receive. It means that the manuscript author has answered Reviewer Questions 1 through 4 successfully.

According to Orwell, "the following rules will cover most cases:

1. Never use a metaphor, simile, or other figure of speech that you are used to seeing in print.
2. Never use a long word where a short one will do.
3. If it is possible to cut a word out, always cut it out.
4. Never use the passive where you can use the active.

5. Never use a foreign phrase, a scientific word, or a jargon word if you can think of an everyday English equivalent.
6. Break any of these rules sooner than say anything outright 'barbarous.'" (p. 170)

Orwell had the good sense to include the sixth rule as a disclaimer. All writers make errors and violate rules, sometimes out of carelessness, sometimes for effect. It is also true that writing for highly specialized journals does require the judicious use of technical language, just as sheep shearers need specialized terms to describe differing grades of wool. However, moderation in the use and the arbitrary, spontaneous creation of specialized vocabulary is certainly warranted in our field. It is refreshing to read an author who states that the subjects in the study are "thinking critically" rather than "realizing greater cognitive gains."

Orwell makes many fine points about the importance of sincerity in thinking and writing. For the prospective social science writer, none are more important than the careful selection and lively use of technical terms. I know of no more rigorous test to apply to a manuscript than to ask if George Orwell would approve. Passing this "test" means the author is thinking straight and writing that way.

References

Green, K., Fine, M. J., & Tollefson, N. (1988). Family systems characteristics and underachieving gifted adolescent males. *Gifted Child Quarterly, 32,* 267–276.

Orwell, G. (1953). Politics and the English language. In G. Orwell (Ed.), *A collection of essays* (pp. 156–171). San Diego: Harcourt, Brace, Jovanovich.

Rica, J. (1984). Learning styles and preferred instructional strategies. *Gifted Child Quarterly, 28,* 121–126.

Robinson, A., Bradley, R., & Stanley, T. D. (in review). Opportunity to achieve: The identification and performance of Black students in a program for the mathematically talented.

Appendix C

The Null Hypothesis and Significance Testing[1]

Formal significance testing begins with the *null hypothesis*. This is a statistical hypothesis that asserts that any differences researchers observe when studying random samples are the result of random (chance) errors created by the random sampling. For instance, suppose a researcher asked a random sample of men from some population and a random sample of women from the same population whether they support legalizing physician-assisted suicide for the terminally ill and found that 51% of the women supported it while only 49% of the men supported it. At first, the researcher might be tempted to report that women are more supportive of this proposition than men are. However, the null hypothesis warns us that the 2-percentage-point difference between women and men may have resulted solely from sampling errors. In other words, there may be no difference between men and women in the population—the researcher may have found a difference because he or she administered the questionnaire to only these two particular samples.

Of course, it is also possible that the men and women in the population are truly different in their opinion on physician-assisted suicide, and the population difference is responsible for the difference between the percentages for the two samples. In other words, the samples may accurately reflect the gender difference in the population. This possibility is called an *alternative hypothesis* (i.e., an alternative to the null hypothesis).

Which hypothesis is correct? It turns out that the only way to answer this question is to test the null hypothesis. If the test indicates that a researcher may reject the null hypothesis, then he or she will be left with only the alternative hypothesis as an explanation. When a researcher rejects the null hypothesis, he or she says that they have identified a *reliable* difference—one that can be relied on because it probably is not just an artifact of random errors.

Through a set of computational procedures that are beyond the scope of this book, a significance test results in a *probability that the null hypothesis is true*. The symbol for this probability is *p*. By conventional standards, when the probability that the null hypothesis is true is as low as or lower than 5 in 100, researchers reject the null hypothesis. (Note that a low probability

---

[1] The authors are grateful to Mildred L. Patten, who wrote this appendix.

means that it is unlikely that the null hypothesis is true. If something is *unlikely* to be true, researchers reject it as a possibility.)

The formal term that researchers use when discussing the rejection of the null hypothesis is *statistical significance*. For example, the following two statements might appear in the results section of a research report:

"The difference between the means for the liberals and conservatives is statistically significant ($p < .05$)."

"The difference between the means for the men and women is not statistically significant ($p > .05$)."

The first statement says that the probability that the null hypothesis is true is less than ($<$) 5 in 100; thus, the null hypothesis is rejected, and the difference is declared to be *statistically significant*. The second statement says that the probability that the null hypothesis is true is greater than ($>$) 5 in 100; thus, the null hypothesis is *not* rejected, and the difference is *not statistically significant*.

In other words, significance tests help researchers make decisions based on the odds that something is true. All individuals do this in their everyday lives. For example, when preparing to cross a busy street, you look at oncoming cars to judge their speed and distance to see if it is safe to cross. If you decide that there is a *low probability* that you will be able to cross the street safely, you *reject* the hypothesis that it is safe to cross the street.